PATCH/WORK VOICES

PATCH/WORK VOICES

The culture and lore of
a mining people

Compiled and written by

Dennis F. Brestensky
Evelyn A. Hovanec
Albert N. Skomra

331.7622
P294

This book was originally made possible by a grant from Fayette Bank and Trust Company, Uniontown, Pennsylvania, as part of its continuing program of civic and community involvement.

Published by the University of Pittsburgh Press, Pittsburgh, Pa. 15260
Copyright © 1991, University of Pittsburgh Press
Eurospan, London
Manufactured in the United States of America

Library of Congress Cataloging-in-Publication Data

Patch/work voices: the culture and lore of a mining people / compiled and
    written by Dennis F. Brestensky, Evelyn A. Hovanec, Albert N. Skomra.
        p.   cm.
    Includes bibliographical references.
    ISBN 0-8229-5460-5 (pbk.)
    1. Coal miners—Pennsylvania—History. I. Brestensky, Dennis. II.
Hovanec, Evelyn A.   III. Skomra, Albert N.
    HD8039.M62U6494   1991
    331.7'622334'09748—dc20   91-50104
                                                                 CIP

A CIP catalogue record for this book is available from the British Library.

This book is dedicated to all those who came and stayed. We are filled with a particularly warm remembrance of those who directly preceded us. Their hard work and persistent dreams made us possible. To our great grandparents, our grandparents, and our parents—thank you.

CONTENTS

PREFACE

In this volume we take a look at the culture of the coal-mining people of southwestern Pennsylvania, a culture whose impact has been enduring, but which is too little known even in its native counties. Today the families remain, but the original culture of the old miners' towns—the patches—often exists only in memory. We believe it is important to salvage for the future these recollections of "a submerged people in whom a boundless vitality survived in the midst of a hemmed-in existence."[1]

In researching this work, which might almost be called an anthology, we interviewed many people. Where possible, we have let them speak for themselves. This, we find, is the best way to capture the authentic voice of the patch and the mine.

Although we interviewed many people and will continue to interview many more, it was impossible to reach everyone and to present every viewpoint. Thus, the reader should not expect the material in this volume to be complete or definitive.

The book concludes with a glossary of terms and a list of selected references for further reading. Much study remains to be done in the lore and the life of the patches, and in the dissemination of the ways of that world into the larger culture—not to mention study of the modern miner and his life. As M. H. Ross has written, "Top level, multi-discipline, compassionate, creative research about coal miners is badly needed. It would do the idealistic academicians and students good to come to know the nation's original hard hats—the mine workers."[2]

---

1. George Korson, *Pennsylvania Songs and Legends* (Baltimore: Johns Hopkins Press, 1949), p. 363.
2. "The Life Style of the Coal Miner—Myth and Reality." *The West Virginia University Magazine* (Summer 1971), p. 32.

ACKNOWLEDGMENTS

If ever a book has been a community project, this one has. It is built upon the words and life experiences of dozens of people. It has been organized and constructed through the efforts of dozens of others. To adequately thank all of these people is a nearly impossible task—yet an effort must be made to do just that. And so, in one resounding voice we give thanks to those dozens who have helped us to make this book a reality.

Photographs on pp. 1, 29, 32–35, and 37 were taken and donated by Daniel Salitrik.

Thanks to Bobby Salitrik, Peggy Triplett, Rose Ann Williams, Carol Kalbaugh, Mary Kay Reilly, and Michael Kalbaugh—our hardworking technical and support personnel.

Thanks to the members of the Penn State organization who have contributed various types of support. They are the Fayette Campus Advisory Board, the Fayette Campus Continuing Education Office, the Fayette Campus Library staff, Joanne Baugh, Hugh Barclay, Stephen Priselac, Albert Bertoni, Harriet Galida, Sharlene Marbury, Mary Jane Duncan, Annabell Bierer, Mildred Hobaugh, Willard McClain, Gilbert Barber, Thomas Knight, Robert Worth Frank, Theodore Kiffer, Joseph Douglas, Thomas Magner, Robert Quinn, and Kenneth Thigpen.

Thanks to the Fayette Bank officers and directors, and especially to Gene Rumisek.

Finally, thanks to those many others who have provided a variety of services, including David Beerbower, Daniel Grimm, Patricia Romito, Sandra Baugh, Carmen Guappone, Daniel Salitrik, Daniel Reilly, and Frederick A. Hetzel and the staff of the University of Pittsburgh Press. Thanks also to the narrators and interviewers whose names appear at the end of this text.

Dennis F. Brestensky
Evelyn A. Hovanec
Albert N. Skomra
Fayette Campus
The Pennsylvania State University

THE COMING

In the eighteenth century, groups of English, Welsh, Scotch-Irish, and German settlers crossed the Alleghenies and settled at the foot of the mountains. They hunted, fished, and farmed the land, and they tamed it. They built their towns—Beeson Town (later Uniontown), Connellsville, Brownsville. They lived off the land and the earth waited. Industrial growth came to the area via its transportation network—the National Road, the Youghiogheny and Monongahela rivers. Iron ore was discovered and iron furnaces sprang up.

And the people diversified.

They farmed and mined and smelted. The Civil War came and went, and industrialization became a powerful force. Power was needed for the machines. Stronger materials were needed to make the machines, and the earth waited. The early inhabitants of the area farmed, mined iron ore, and smelted, but coal was in the earth. Coal was a form of power and the earth became restless. Some decided to use the earth's power and to mine its coal, not for domestic purposes, as early families in the area had always done, but for industrial purposes. It was discovered that this coal, the coal of the Pittsburgh seam, particularly in the Connellsville region, was extremely good for coking and steel making.

And so it began.

To relieve the earth of its coal, people were needed, and the original inhabitants were too few in number for the largeness of the task. The word went out, and the migration from the corners of the Western world to this area began. It was a migration which would take decades for completion and which would bring together an array of differing peoples.

They came.

They came here, from the late 1800s on, for a variety of reasons—to be with families, to provide for the necessities of life, to ensure better social conditions, but above all they came because of a need, because of a desire for better economic opportunities for themselves and for their families. They came—more English, more Welsh, more Irish, more Scotch, more Germans. They came—the Slovaks, the Poles, the Yugoslavians, the Russians, the Hungarians, the Ruthenians, the Italians, the Blacks. They all came to work within the earth, and they stayed.

Through the years these people adapted to a new existence and, in the process, produced a culture which was a unique blend of ethnic and industrial attitudes, customs, and practices of both Europe and America. Their lives have become a part of the history of the bituminous coal industry, and it seems only fitting that an attempt be made to chronicle a few of their stories.

The people who came

WHY THEY CAME—WHY THEY MINED

Mr. Jerry Schuessler, of German background, suggested that many of the earliest miners of the area came because of relatives who lived in the area. His own father came to Westmoreland County from Pittsburgh during the depression years of the 1890s. He got a job at the Morewood Mine. From there the family finally migrated to Bittner. As for his own reason for going into the mines: "My dad worked in a coal mine, and if you lived in a patch, you naturally went into the coal mine. Kids in those days [around 1920]—if the father worked in the mine—they went into the coal mine. Never any question about it! When you'd get to be seventeen or eighteen years old, you went into the mines, and all of your brothers went in too."

Mrs. Peggy Triplett indicated that her father, Mr. Herbert Evans, never intended to be a miner. He came here from England to be with his mother, who had migrated here earlier to marry a miner. When he got here, he needed work. He went into the mines for economic reasons.

Mr. Paul Vrobel, of Slovak descent, discussed the migration of the Slavs to the mines in this way: "In my opinion, the Slavs [all of the Eastern European peoples] who came between the 1880s and the 1920s came to the mines because they didn't have a profession, and they needed a job. They had heard this was a land of milk and honey." When Mr. Vrobel was asked if he thought those early immigrants were sorry that they came, he answered, "No, they never said they were disappointed." His wife, Mrs. Ann Plevich Vrobel, chimed in with the remembrance of her father, a Croatian immigrant. She said that she once asked him if he wanted to go back to Europe for a vacation. His answer was, "What do I want over there?" Mr. Vrobel went on to explain that "a lot of those people came with tags on their coats. They couldn't read or write or understand English. The tag gave their name and where they were going. And they were shipped to this area, and someone would meet them — usually relatives."

Mr. Leonard Santella came to this area from Italy in 1921. He came to southwestern Pennsylvania because he had a brother living in the Masontown area. When asked why he decided to leave Italy, he explained, "I was all through World War I [in the Italian Army], and then when I got home things were pretty bad. I had to leave. I had gotten married, and there was not much food. We could do nothing. So I thought to myself, 'I better leave.' And, I left my wife and baby over there." Later he managed to save enough money to bring his family here, and they settled in the Gates area. He indicated that he worked in the mines because that was where he could get a job.

Blacks came to the area for two reasons, economic and social. They came during two different time periods: prior to the strikes of the 1920s and during the strikes of the 1920s. Prior to 1920 they came of their own volition to better themselves. During the strikes they came—unknown to them—as part of an attempt to break the strikes. One story of a Black family coming under its own volition was told by Mr. Howard Dantzler. According to Mr. Dantzler, his grandfather, Mr. Greene Dantzler, had been an unpaid teacher in Alabama who had found it necessary to work in the three-foot coal mines of Carbon Hill, Alabama, just to insure survival for his family. His son, Henry Dantzler, followed his father into the Carbon Hill Mine, but decided that the social conditions that surrounded him were not to his liking. He migrated to southwestern Pennsylvania during World War I and found a job in the nine-foot coal mines of the area. He then established his family here. Like most mining families, they moved around the area to various mines and patches until they finally settled in the Footedale area. His three oldest sons followed him into the mines.

Social conditions and economic necessity seem to be at the root of every story. Others who were asked why they worked in the mines only emphasized these points:

"My father [Stephen Kovach] said that he began to work in the mine at the age of fourteen. His father died; so he had to go to work to support the family."

(Narrated by Johanna Swetz)

"My father's father died so he had to go to work at the age of eleven or twelve. He worked as a trapper boy and later as a miner."

(Narrated by Andrew Hovanec)

"I was forced to go [to the mines] because my dad was failing in health, and we had a large family of ten."

(Narrated by Alex Whoolery)

"[I went to the mines] because we had a big family, and I was the oldest of fourteen."

(Narrated by Bill Burke)

"It was a job, and I was looking for work, and I decided I had to make the best of it."

(Narrated by Mike Gugar)

And so the earth and the people—of necessity—came together here in southwestern Pennsylvania. The people mined, they lived, they fought, they laughed, they struggled, they died, and they persevered in this land.

WORK

Buddies hand loading coal wagon

Work in the mines has never been considered easy, but most miners who worked in the pre-mechanical years would agree with the assertion that "it was all hard work, buddy, let me tell you." Stanley Machinsky remembers that "in the twenties a miner might have had to work fifteen or sixteen hours, and only made a dollar." And, in the thirties, says Ray Nicklow, "we worked ten or twelve hours for maybe four to five dollars, and if you got a bad place or slate, maybe you made three dollars. You punched in at 5 a.m. You got up and went to work at 4 a.m. —by the time you changed clothes it was 5 o'clock. You'd work all day and come out at 4 p.m. or 5 p.m. In the wintertime, you'd go in the dark and come home in the dark."

WORK ENVIRONMENT

Many things were a direct part of a miner's work environment. There were his tools and equipment, his buddy, the horses, and the daily cage trip and bath.

Tools

In the pre-mechanical mines, men dug coal with picks and shovels, and they loaded it into wagons that were pulled by horses or mules. To prepare coal to be shot with dynamite, a person hand-drilled holes with an auger and breast plate. Using a tamping stick, he would put the dynamite sticks and primer stick in the hole and tamp it with non-combustible material, such as clay or rock dust.

Other tools used were a slate bar to pry down loose rock; a spiking hammer to drive little spikes in the rails when laying track; an ax to prepare posts and timber; a sledge hammer to pry down heavy rock and break it up into small pieces so you could "gob" it; a two-man saw to cut posts and timber; and a file to sharpen the auger bit.

(Reconstructed from the accounts of Sam Calderone and Mike Gugar)

The Anton Lamp

The first manufactured pit lamps used in the early United States mines were invented and produced in southwestern Pennsylvania by the Anton

Stephen A. Peters and Sunshine Lamps

Brothers, whose family came from Bavaria and settled in Monongahela in 1849.

From 1874 to 1918, John, George, Chris, and Fred Anton operated their lamp factories in the Mon Valley. Their lamps were commercially known as the Anton lamps, but most miners called them "sunshine lamps" because they brought light to the dark underground pits.

As the picture shows, the lamps resembled little coffee pots or syrup pitchers. On the back was a hook that fastened onto the front of the miner's cap.

Stephen Anton Peters, a Fayette County native and the great-grandson of John Anton, has several of these lamps in his collection. According to him, "The lamps were made of brass, copper, tin plate, or a combination of these materials, and had the trademarks of a star emblem, a globe, and an eagle." The rarest of the lamps, he adds, "are those with the emblems of the Statue of Liberty, which were manufactured in very limited quantities."

In describing the operating procedures of the Anton lamp, Steve Peters says: "A wick in the spout would be lit with a match. The insulated air spout had the effect of carrying the heat from the flame down the spout into the solid paraffin fuel called sunshine. This heat melted the fuel and made capillary action possible."

Although the sunshine lamp is now a collector's item, its invention by the Anton Brothers of Mon Valley is a good example of how southwestern Pennsylvania played a leading role in the development of coal mining in the United States in the early twentieth century.

Buddy System

Choosing to work with the same man everyday and alternating the work with him was known as the buddy system. This technique of working was encouraged for two reasons: (1) it often resulted in faster, more efficient work; (2) it provided each man with immediate help if he became sick or injured.

Albert Murray describes the buddy system this way: "Two men would work together for years. It was nice; maybe one would shovel left hand, and one would shovel right hand in the wagon. If you took two right-handed men or two left-handed men, they'd have an awful time of it. So naturally, when you got a buddy you could work with, you tried to stick with him. And whenever you got a buddy like that and you'd get in a water hole, why, he would trade places with you, too. You used to put tags on the wagons and every other one was yours and every other one was your buddy's."

Use of Horses

In the early days of mining, coal was hauled by horses pulling one or two wooden or metal wagons at a time on wooden rails (later iron rails were used) made from two-by-fours. The horses and wagons were guided by a person called a driver. Each driver had his own horse supplied by the company. He always had the same horse. When the driver was off from work, his horse didn't work. The driver had six or seven places to haul coal from. For each loaded wagon he pulled out, the driver returned one empty. The men were paid by the number of wagons loaded. One wagon was equal to about fifty bushels, although many were larger.

(Reconstructed from the accounts of Andrew Billek and Steve Ludrosky)

Entering and Leaving

On either end of the day were the trip down in the cage (although some walked in or used a mantrip) and, for some, the ritual of the bathhouse after work. One miner described entering a mine via a cage: "They had an elevator, operated by steam [later by electricity]. When it started down, your bucket almost went up to your shoulders, and when he stopped down at the bottom, let me tell you, your bucket just about went to the floor."

When the day was completed, according to Ray Nicklow, "you'd come out black, dusty, and dirty. Your clothes would be full of coal dust. Your mouth and hair would be full of dust. You had a bathhouse and a rack with a basket on it. You would undress and take a shower—sometimes the bathhouse was cold, sometimes the water was cold in the winter. You'd shower and then you got your basket and dressed and put your work clothes in the basket. You had a long chain on the basket and you'd pull it up and the basket would hook."

WORK PRACTICES

There was a variety of work practices in the coal mines, especially the pre-mechanized mines of the early twentieth century, which were vital to the safety and well-being of the individual miner as well as his buddies. As apprentice miners developed mining skills, they quickly learned these techniques and practiced them routinely as the necessity arose.

Sounding the roof

Sounding the Roof

One of the more basic of these practices was the technique known as "sounding." John Hustosky, a retired coal miner, recalls his first days in the mine and explains the custom of "sounding the roof." "Well, instructions given to me when I first went in was to do whatever my buddy told me to do. I was inexperienced, and he was an experienced miner, and I was to do what he told me to do. The main thing was to keep our place posted, well posted, timbered—and we would sound our roof to see that it sounded properly. You held one hand up against the roof with your fingers spread out, and would tap the roof with the end of your pick handle. A hollow sound means the roof is beginning to pull loose. If the sound was solid, the roof was all right. If you found any conditions where the coal began to peel off or fall, you had to stop loading and correct the condition."

Setting a Pick

Another practice essential to a miner's productivity and general well-being was "setting the pick." A miner's pick was fixed on a wooden pick handle to form the letter T. It was imperative that the pick (metal part) be horizontal to the handle (wooden stock) so that there was no wasted effort on the miner's part, and his work, therefore, was less tiring. After the miner swung his pick in an arc, he would turn the pick handle in his hands as he drew back so as to strike the coal face with the opposite end of his pick. If the pick was not "true" (exactly horizontal to the handle), the second strike would miss the spot he had hit before. The net result would be wasted effort since he would have to swing again to accomplish the task of digging out the coal. Miners knew the importance of a well-balanced, or "true" pick, and so for many of them the practice of "setting a pick" was carried out with the solemnity and attention to detail of a religious rite.

Many miners used their off days to tend to their various hand tools, and many attended to this routine necessity with the devotion and air of artistic craftsmanship. The ideal time to set a pick was a warm day with bright sunlight. The process was carried out, generally, in the back yard just off the back porch. The first step was to remove the old, worn, or broken pick handle from the pick. This could be done by hammering, cutting, burning, or drilling out the stump of the old handle. Once this was accomplished, the new pick was set on the handle and the first of two wedges—a wooden one—was driven in the pick handle. Now came the important part — "setting the pick." In order to set the pick, the miner placed the butt end of the handle against some solid, vertical object. This was usually the box or stool upon which he was seated. He then held the pick handle in his hands, and as he braced the handle butt against his seat, he struck a semicircle on the ground with one end of the pick point. He then turned the pick over and repeated the process with the other pointed end of the pick. If the two arcs he had scribed were off, he then adjusted his pick on its handle until both points of the pick cast a line in exactly the same arc. When this had been accomplished, he drove another wedge (metal) crosswise to the wood wedge to secure the pick on its handle. Once the job of setting the pick was accomplished, the miner could sit back knowing that some part of his job would be a little easier now that he had a properly balanced tool.

(Reconstructed from the account of Louis J. Skomra)

Shooting a Cut

"FIRE IN THE HOLE!" Mining law required that the shotfirer shout these words three times before he shot his cut. Shooting a cut was the practice of dynamiting a section of coal so that it could be loaded into coal cars and eventually brought to the surface for transport and use.

The process began by having two holes about 1½" in diameter drilled into the coal at the face (vertical wall of coal to be mined). These holes were started about a foot from the bottom (floor) and about four feet from each rib (side). They were drilled on a slight downward angle to a depth of about four feet. (In the early days of mining these holes were drilled by hand. Later, they were machine drilled.) The holes were then plugged with wooden plugs in preparation for the cutting process.

Then the cutting machine (somewhat like a huge chain saw) was brought to the face where the cutting operator made four cuts with his bar or blade. The first cut was made horizontally on the very top of the face about ten to twelve feet across and nine feet deep. The cutter then made two vertical cuts on each side of the section from top to bottom. Each vertical cut was also nine feet deep. The final cut was a vertical nine foot deep cut right through the center of the coal block or section. When the cutting was finished, the coal face resembled a huge E lying on its side with the open ends down.

The shotfirer would then come in, remove the wooden plugs, and place ten sticks of dynamite in each hole. The tenth stick in each hole held a detonator, a nine-foot piece of shotfire wire (much like a doorbell wire) with a brass electric charge on the end. To set the detonator, the shotfirer made two holes in each of the final sticks of dynamite. The first hole was made in the middle and the other hole in one end. Then the detonator was placed in the center hole and also threaded around and brought into the end hole. The purpose for this was that in case of a misfire (charge does not explode) the shotfirer could retrieve the dynamite and detonator. After the tenth stick of dynamite with its detonator was placed in each hole, stemming (a clay composition) was placed in back of the tenth stick, and the entire hole was closed off with stemming. Since the shotfirer was only permitted to shoot one charge at a time, he usually tied the shotfire wire of the detonator that was not being set off to some object nearby, e.g., a timber leg. This was to enable him to locate the wire in the debris after the first charge was set off.

The final stage of the process involved attaching his shotfire cable to the detonator. The shotfirer then unwound his shotfire wire its full length (125 feet) and made his traditional calls—"FIRE IN THE HOLE!" Having determined that the area was clear of people and/or animals, he electrically (with a battery) set off his charges one at a time. Both shots generally produced thirty tons of coal for loading. This account represents one of several shooting methods used in the coal mines.

(Reconstructed from the account of Louis J. Skomra)

Four-pole timbering

Timbering

Coal mining is a relentless task of extracting coal from the seam in the earth by tunneling through it. Once a section of coal has been removed, supports must be erected to keep the roof of the mined out area from collapsing on the workers as they mine ahead. The process of supporting the roof before the advent of roof bolts was called timbering. This was ordinarily a two-man operation and began with the timbermen setting their timber jack directly below the section of the roof to be timbered. The timber jack was essentially a five- to eight-foot screw type jack with a cradle or Y on the upper end. The jack was set on its base end, and some coal and/or debris was placed around the base so that the jack would stand erect by itself. Then the two timbermen would carry a cross bar into the section. This was a piece of round, rough lumber roughly twelve feet long. The two men placed the timber on the cradle of the jack, and while one man operated the jack, his buddy grabbed one end of the timber and angled the other end up against the roof on a slant. When the timber was finally positioned against the roof and space was left between the timber and the roof for lagging, the men then set the legs under the timber. The legs were posts which were placed under each end of the timber for support after the jack was removed. Since timbers or crossbars were placed six feet apart, lagging was used to span the distance between timbers. The lagging was eight feet in length, and each one extended beyond the timber. The final effect was a grid or criss-cross pattern of timber on the roof. After everything was set, the timbermen drove wooden wedges between the legs and the crossbar to firm them against the roof. Once this was completed, the jack was removed and the men started loading coal. The process of timbering as described took two men about a half-hour.

(Reconstructed from the account of Louis J. Skomra)

THOSE DAMNED ANIMALS!

According to reports, a variety of animal life, large and small, inhabited the mines of southwestern Pennsylvania. There have been reports of finding snakes, raccoons, mice, and even an occasional dog or cat in them. For example, Mr. Asa Herring reports that the ghost of a haunted mine turned out to be a dog who had gotten lost in the mine and decided to howl for help. John Hustosky recalls catching a small pig in the Smock mine. However, by far most of the animal anecdotes reported concern the exploits and personalities of three prominent animals of the mines— the horses and mules who provided the transportation power of the pre-mechanical mine, and the rats, who served in several capacities.

Generally, horse anecdotes recount the strength and dependability of the animal. At times they relate to the care and feeding of the horse. For example, Mr. Andrew Hovanec suggested that feeding a horse tobacco will kill his worms. Once in a while, a story concerning the tragedy of a well-liked horse or the peculiarities of a particular horse might be recounted. For example, there was the case of a Paddy horse who objected to being spit upon or having a finger shaken at him. However, the characteristics of the horse that seemed to be valued most by the miners—in addition to his strength and dependability—were the perseverance and resourcefulness of the animal.

One story is told by Mr. Leonard Santella, an eighty-year-old retired miner who spent his life in the Gates area. According to Mr. Santella, water had broken through from the abandoned Puritan mine and was rapidly enveloping large parts of the Gates mine. He and several of his buddies managed to escape, but a driver had been forced to abandon his horse. "Water was up to the roof already. So the driver left the horse there. He couldn't get him through. . . . The horse stayed [in the flooded mine] for nine days. Now this horse to live chewed the bark off all of the posts that we had in there. He chewed all of these posts. And he broke a water pipe with his hoof. The pipe had clean water. So he had this water, and he ate the bark. Now there was a big dip in the coal in this part of the mine. So the flood water drained down into the dip. The horse, he stayed on the high point and let the water go through his legs. He stayed there for nine days. And we thought we'd find him dead. But he broke that valve, the water was coming up—fresh water—he drank that water and ate that bark, and he lived that way for nine days."

Stories of mules, on the other hand, tend to emphasize the stubborness, meanness, and quick intelligence of the animal. Often when the story is being recounted there is a humorous, affectionate glint in the man's eye and a respect for the aggressiveness and competitiveness of the animal. In the competition to be master, it is important that one of the opponents should outsmart the other. In some of these stories the man wins; in others the mule wins.

Mr. Joseph Rerko of Fairchance recounted a story that he had gotten from an "old-timer." "This old fella about seventy-five years old told me that he'll never forget the coal mine as long as he lives and especially this one mule. He says this incident occurred when he was a kid, and he was working in Sewickley coal. It's about five feet deep. He says he asked for a job driving because he was too skinny to load coal. He was just a little fellow. Well, the boss looked at him and started to laugh when he asked for a job. Then the boss said, 'Sure, I'll give you a job.' So they gave him this mule, and the boss told this guy, 'You go ahead and put this mule to work in there. I'll give you one digger. That'll be enough for you to haul from—just one man.' So this guy goes in and hooks up this mule to the wagon, and he calls him by name—Jack. And he said this mule just stood there and pranced from one side to the other, from one side to the other, from one side of the rib to the other side of the rib. But he wouldn't move. So this guy says he just stood there, and then he beat that mule, and then he beat him again. And that mule just turned his head a little bit and looked at him and still kept prancing and kicking at the tail chain. This mule was getting a real sweat on now. So this guy says to himself, 'There's only one thing I can do with this mule.' He had this carbide lamp on him and a carbide flask to carry the carbide. And he thought about that carbide. So he petted the mule, and he talked to him, and he laid his hand on the mule's rump and felt that he was all wet. So this guy took out some of this carbide in his hand, and talked to that mule and the mule raised up his tail a little bit. And then the guy dropped some of that carbide down on his behind—you know, on his hind end. Well, when you get dampness and carbide together it creates a gas, and then it starts

That damn mule

to burn. It'll burn your flesh. So he said after he did this, that mule all at once started to switching his tail, going from one side to another. Then he said he hollered at the mule, and he said, 'My oh my—that mule took off and never stopped running until he got outside, and he must have run at least a half mile even after he got outside. As a matter of fact that mule almost ran into the side of the tipple. He was going hell bent on election.' Well, finally they got him stopped and the tipple boss laughed and said to the guy, 'How'd you ever get that mule started? Nobody ever got that mule started ever before.' This guy looked at him and said, 'I think I've got the secret.' Well this guy hooked up that mule again and took him back. He said that mule didn't want to go, but he finally got him back in. By this time his digger was getting upset, and he said, 'Come on boy, you'd better get these wagons out of here, or I'm not going to make anything today.' So this fella hollered at Jack again, but Jack wouldn't move again. Old Jack just stood there switching his tail. So this fella said he thought about that carbide again. But he said, 'I didn't have to use that carbide a second time. All I had to do was take that carbide can and rattle it a little and, My God, that old mule took right out of there.' This fella said that he worked with that mule a long time and that was the only way that he ever got that mule to go. He said, 'I drove for two men after that, and all I ever had to do was rattle that can.'"

Reverend Andrew Wilson, a retired, eighty-five-year-old coal miner and minister, recounted another mule story in an interview conducted by Melvin Nicklow. His story suggests that the mule sometimes scores a point but that, in the end, man is the smarter of the pair. "I used to drive a mule. I had an old mule named Toby. That rascal, he would kick. Old Toby just kept kicking that leg. At one time I had another mule and one time I was going down to the main haulage with a trip of coal. We had a low place to go through. Water just stood in there. Well, that mule would just get into the deepest water, and then the wagons would get hard to pull, and so he would just kick himself loose from his tail chain and take off back to where we fed him. And he'd just leave me sitting there in the water with my trip of coal. That old mule one time stuck his head in a manhole. Then when I'd go to one side to try to get hold of him to lead him up, he'd turn his heels on me. Then I'd go to the other side, and he'd do the same thing. He could see my light, and he just kept ahead of me. So you know how I finally got him out of there? I went down on this one side and took off my light and put it down there. He thought I was still standing there. Then I went on the other side of him and gave him a slap with a shovel of coal, and he took out from there so fast. Well, that's one time I fooled him."

But the mule wasn't always outsmarted. There were times when he won the competition. The following story was told by Mr. Asa Herring. "Once I saw a mule going down the hill one time, and he was an ornery, dirty, old white mule. And the driver had decided to try to kill him. He had three empties in front of him and three empties behind him, and there was nothing on the side. There was no room on the side. No place to go. And the driver let these wagons go, and they came down that track and that old mule just up and jumped into the empty wagons in front of him. And he was riding the wagon then. That mule was smarter than the driver."

The third animal who frequented the deep was not loved or admired as was the horse, nor did he share friendly competition with man as did the mule (unless it was competition for food), but he certainly got his share of attention, and he did have his functions. The rat often served as an early warning safety device. Many of the older miners report the belief that if a rat decided to leave a place, then the men would be wise to follow. It was believed that the keener hearing of the rat, plus the fact that he was usually closer to the coal and ground, gave the rat a clearer indication of the earth working or of possible falls or trouble. Mr. Charles Billy relates that a coal miner was never to kill a rat in the mine, for three good reasons. First, one will never find a rat where there is blackdamp. Second, a rat is never found in a section where gas is evident—the rats will run toward a spot where the air is good. Third, rats can tell if the roof is unstable. Rats were rather predictable safety devices in the early days. The feeling about them today, however, is a little mixed. Some miners report their worth as safety devices; others report finding a lot of dead rats after an explosion. Apparently, their noses were not keen enough.

Although many of the miners did not like the rats, nearly all learned to tolerate them, and there are even a few rat stories around. Reverend Andrew Wilson reports that once he had his bucket sitting on the gob and that a big rat came in with his muddy feet and got up on top of his bucket. In the meantime, Reverend Wilson had gone to get some materials that he needed to do a job. "When I came in with this steel tie, this rat came at me. I sure got out of there. I threw that steel tie at that rat and knocked the leg out from under the cross timber and that timber came down. It hit me on the head and knocked me down. No more! I'm not chasing rats no more." Rev. Wilson related this story with a bit of a chuckle.

Among many of the older miners, it was a custom to feed the rats. The rats became dinner companions, although not always welcome dinner companions. Sometimes the rats were not in the mood to wait to be fed by a friendly miner, and they would just help themselves. It was reported that a big rat could get the food out of a miner's closed bucket in two ways. First, he could just knock the bucket over, hoping that the fall or jar would open it. The second method was more ingenious. The rat simply wrapped his tail around the ring on the top of the bucket and then pulled off the lid. If neither of these methods worked, he just had to wait for his dinner partner to share with him. Ray Nicklow described the rats as "pretty tame." He went on to say that "if you'd sit there and eat and if you didn't watch, they'd come almost up to where you were for something to eat."

Whatever the feelings of the older miners toward rats, though, nearly all agreed that they did have at least two serious functions. They did provide a miner with a warning of danger in the pre-mechanical days— and any warning of danger was important. Also, they were good garbage disposals. They helped to clean up the wastes of the mine whether it was left-over lunch scraps or the wastes of the horses and mules.

LABOR STRIFE

One of the major outgrowths of America's industrial process has been the labor strikes—a work stoppage by laborers as a means of securing redress for grievances or injustices. Here in southwestern Pennsylvania, the coal industry experienced many long, bitter, and costly (to both labor and management) strikes. Of these strikes, the one most vividly remem-

York Run Mine, circa 1912

bered by those who lived through it is the 1921-22 strike. What follows are personal reflections on this event.

"It happened during the 1921-22 strike which lasted about a year and a half. Even though there was work available, the men had to call the strike for better pay and for better working conditions. So the families of the men that had been refusing to go to work had been evicted from their [company] homes. They were given ten days' notice, prior to eviction, but if they didn't move out, the sheriff came and moved them out.

"So we had a farm, and we took some of them in. Our property wasn't too far from the York Run patch. And the sheriff would get these people's furniture on a truck, and they would just dump them right on the ground, on the border of my father's property. And these folks had to go and carry all their things by hand onto our property. All these things—stoves, whatever—they were all carried.

"Well, anyhow, this one day, it was very sad, there were four families that came to our home, and this one family had ten children. The only thing that my father could do is put two families in our barn and two families in our house with us. This was crowded, but our parents put up with it. In our barn was the family with ten children, and the other family had four, which made it sixteen in all. The barn looked just like a hospital ward with all these beds set up. The next day there were two more families that came on our farm. They pitched tents, and the families lived temporarily in these tents. Then the men got busy in the following days and put up one-room huts, you might as well say, just enough to put a coal stove in and put in a table and chairs, and this was where these folks would cook and eat. They also put up small brick ovens in our yard, and these women would take turns about in baking their bread. They would also pick wild raspberries and make jelly, and this is how these folks tried to live during this period.

"The strike started in about mid-May of 1921, and this is when these evicted families came to our farm. Also during this period, there were folks in Pittsburgh that heard about all these striking families that had this rough life. They felt sorry for these families and would offer their children jobs. There would be children taken from ages eleven, twelve, thirteen, and fourteen, and this one particular time, I remember, there was a huge truck, and all these children were put on it. They were taken to Pittsburgh where the girls would get light housework and help with the dishes, and the boys would be given yard work and helping with different chores that were suitable for boys. And this is how the families made out. And when these children came home, it was already time to go to school. They would get a little bit of money for their help in Pittsburgh, and the work gave them some money for school clothes. So, it was a very sad time, and I remember quite a few of these women just shed tears."

(Narrated by Tekla Hensh Skomra)

"It was 1922 when the coal miners decided that they would strike to try to get a better way of life and wages and other conditions. And naturally, living in a coal camp or coal town, whichever way you want it, why they would ask the men to work and if they refused to work, why you couldn't live in the town. You would come home, and they'd drive up with a horse and wagon ... and they would load all your furniture up on this wagon and haul it out to a country road some place, and take it and throw it off the wagon and leave it there. And then the union officials would get another horse and wagon from a farmer, and they would come out and load your furniture up on this wagon and take it out to a central area, a camp, and they used the old army tents—W.W. I surplus—and one family could fit in there. But it was very crowded because in our tent—we lived in one there for about eight months; all during one winter up until spring and summer of the following year—we lived in Mather, Pennsylvania—our whole family lived in that one tent. We had two beds, a kitchen stove, a cupboard, and trunks. In other words, all the family's worldly possessions were in this one tent. We got thrown out of the patch because our father refused to work—he called it scabbing.

"Another thing, at night when you were in this camp, why the company would have a great big search light up on top of the tipple, and they would direct one of these big search lights on to the camp and leave it there all night so that they could see what was going on. They had armed guards around their towns. They even had police, some called them yellow dogs, some, Coal and Iron Police. They rode on horseback, and they would guard the company property. They would ride around at night to make sure none of the strikers would come and do some damage to the coal mines with explosives and stuff like that. . . . There were some pretty good fights down around the train depot outside the company property. The union officials would go down to pick up the mail for the camp of strikers and the company would send their guards to pick up supplies, and every once in a while, it would become violent and fists would fly and people would be beaten. The whole strike lasted a year and a half."

(Narrated by Paul Vrobel)

"When I was smaller, we lived in Alicia where they had the coke ovens, and they had strike breakers. And the people that were out on strike were all out in tents in the dead of winter. And you had the Coal and Iron Police who would patrol back and forth, trying to keep peace. Then they brought the strike breakers in, and there were fights and all kinds of stone throwing. And the people sat out all winter and lived in them tents till they got back to work. The company hired the Coal and Iron Police."

(Narrated by Ray Nicklow)

Unfortunately, violence was a by-product of mining strikes.

"Some of the scabs or Coal and Iron Police would use war tactics on the strikers. When we were on the picket line, there were two union men shot and killed. There were deputies in a car going through. They just shot at the picket line; they didn't aim at anyone in particular. There was no way to prove who did it. The police were just as bad. They had to be for the company. There were cars turned over and everything. It was like a war! They [union men] turned a superintendent's car over on a bridge. He got out of there, and he ran!"

(Narrated by Albert Murray, retold by Debi Sabo)

One of the outcomes of the labor strife in the mines was the unionization of the miners.

"Any miner in the twenties and thirties remembers well the organization of the union. There was an uprising in 1922 that was quickly quieted, and it wasn't until after the 1929 depression, about 1932, that the strikes started [again]. The two opposing forces were the unionmen and the brotherhoods. Outbreaks ranged from individual to gang and army type fights. Some of the scuffles were fatal. My uncle was in favor of the union, and he said you had to be careful in not letting the 'company' discover your involvement. If the 'company' found that you were a union radical, they would, without any notice, go to your house and throw your furniture and belongings onto the street, leaving you without a home or job.

"On many occasions, the 'mini battles' lasted for three and four days until the National Guard, or Militia as the miners called it, was called in to squelch the fights. My uncle was involved in many fights, but he never received any serious injuries. By 1936, the company realized the union was here to stay. The miner's hours were shortened and his pay increased. He now earned enough money to feel his work was worthwhile."

(Narrated by Stanley Machinsky; retold by Kimberly Collins)

DISASTER AND NEAR DISASTER

"They used to blow those whistles. They used to have a big whistle when there would be an accident. In every patch that I lived in if there'd be an accident... they'd just blow that whistle for hours and hours and hours. When there'd be an accident or an explosion, everybody would run when they'd hear that whistle. Down to the mine. Oh, it was almost like an air raid siren, only louder."

(Narrated by Ray Nicklow)

Many whistles have blown over the years, each marking a disaster or near disaster. And although we may no longer blow that whistle to bring the people down to the mines, we still alert them via the media whenever disaster or near disaster strikes in the mines. Men died before, and men still die. They die from many things just as they always have. Accidents still do occur. Most of these mine disasters, near disasters, and accidents are immediately involved with one or a combination of three things: the earth, fire, or water. It is true that today mechanical accidents occur more often. But it is also true that today the same three nemeses still plague the miner. The four cases that are narrated here share a sameness. Each describes an element of life that each miner and his family must accept as a part of the mining tradition: the possibility of injury, disaster, or near disaster. The whistle still blows, at least figuratively.

The Earth

"In 1954 this place that fell in was three cuts out at the intersection. And I went in, and I shot the upper shots — the top. I came back out, and as I was coming out, there was a big lip that came down. That jar, that shot loosened it. And it came down and buried me right there. I don't remember it hitting me. Like I said, for a few seconds it must have knocked me out because I don't remember. It just seems like you're standing up, and the next thing you know—you're laying down with all of this stuff on top of you. I would say there was close to fifty ton that came down, not counting the smaller stuff. But there was one piece there that was twenty-six feet by eighteen feet and over two feet thick laying on top of me from the waist down. But I recall, after a few minutes there I came to my senses that they were all running. Everybody running. I started hollering for them to come back and help me. It's a frightening experience. You just look up—I pushed a piece of slate off my face and looked up — and there was a piece that weighed three or four or five hundred pounds. And it was gapped open six or eight inches. Just waiting to come. I figured if it came down, it would cut my head right off. Then one guy said, 'Let's get him out.' He said, 'You watch it, and I'm going to start digging.' So they dug me out."

(Narrated by Chuck Hudek)

Fire

"I lived in Pitgas. I was about twelve years old [this occurs around 1930]. And they had an explosion and the mine caught fire. Well, they called my brother and dad in right away, and everybody went down to the mine. All us kids, my mother, the rest of the family. We all went down to the mine. They had set up tables and coffee and everybody waited. And that fire— it took a whole week to get that fire out. It burned up half the mine. The gas in the mine and blackdamp — they caused an explosion with a fire.

And there were some killed, and we'd stand there and watch 'em bring 'em out all covered over. And their wives would be there and children. And there were some of them burned up. They brought 'em out. They were completely burned up. And it's an awful feeling to stand outside and watch. We stayed down there a whole week in shifts watching them bring out the bodies. They had a big building where they took them and put them in."

(Narrated by Ray Nicklow)

DUNBAR, PA., MARCH 24. — The dead have been wrested from their untimely tomb and all that remains now is to accord a Christian burial to the miners who met their fate in the Hill Farm mine at Dunbar, June 16, 1890. Yesterday the bodies of twenty-three of the miners were found and today they will be brought to the surface for burial. . . .

The struggle for life of the entombed miners was as terrible as it was brief. They were suffocated—not burned or starved—and it is improbable that any lived longer than half an hour. There is an unwritten law of protection among miners by which they rush together at the sound of an explosion, impelled by a common instinct of self-preservation, for together they stand a better chance of fighting for freedom. So was it with the Hill Farm victims. When found they were huddled together in flat No. 10, showing that they had rushed deeper into the mine and that a moment later a scorching breath of death filled the flat, choking their lungs, bursting their veins and striking them to the earth to linger in horrible torture a few moments and then to die. . . .

After two weeks' work the searchers were compelled to abandon the work for a time till the fire, which followed the explosion, could be extinguished. The mine was then sealed up and flooded to subdue the fire, after which months were required to clear the mine of water and tons of collected debris produced by the fire. . . .

(Reported in *The United Mine Workers' Journal*
for Thursday, March 31, 1892)

Water

"I was working at Gates [this occurs around 1922]. There was an old mine, Puritan, back of McClellandtown. That mine was full of water, and they knew it. So they marked how much coal they could take, and they'd leave seventy-five or one hundred feet of coal that they couldn't bother. This was nine- or ten-foot coal. So everyone hogged a little of it. So the machine man was cutting at the bottom. Whenever they were cutting that night, they heard a lot of noise. So they knew the water was on the other side. That machine man saw the water start to leak. They took off and went. That water filled up all day. The water broke in from the Puritan mine. It come down through Edenborn then down to Gates. So the pitboss wanted to save part of the mine. So he wanted to build a stopping. We came to the main line [haulage], but we couldn't finish the stopping. The water was pushing all the air and the gas. The supply man had come in and told us the water was coming in. The boss told him to go out. He tried to go out. But before he got 1,000 feet the roof was there, and he couldn't go no more. He came back. We thought we could go out through the north [part of the mine]. But the water was up to the roof in places already. So we were still building the stopping. These two or three men were finishing the stopping on the main line, and I was on the other side. Everything they lifted, the air took because the water was pushing all the air and gas. I got scared. But one of the bosses said we'd go out through Lambert. One of the guys ran away. He was scared. When he got outside, the pitboss asked where he came from, and he told the boss we were finishing the stopping and were going to go out through Lambert. 'O My God,' he said and he ran. The water from one side was penetrating to the other part of the mine. He [the pitboss] had to walk through a lot of water. He hollered — 'Jesus Criminy, all of the gas is back there. When you close that stopping you're not going to go fifty feet because that gas is going to choke you. It's all back there.' So, lucky he came. So we tried to close the hole in the stopping and went back to the other side [of it]. Just as soon as we finished, one of the boys took a walk, and he said the water is starting to come down the hill, not too far. I said, 'This is going too far.' I said, 'I'm going. Let's get out of here.' I walked fast. I was young then. Me and another Italian boy started walking. We were going to come out of the other part of the mine. Everything was connected, and I knew that mine all over. When we got to one place there was a line [electric or telephone] along that haulage about seven or eight inches from the roof. But the water was so high already that all I could see was the light on the other side. And I said, 'There's a light over there — let's go.' So we took hold of the wire, and we went about 1,000 to 2,000 feet on that wire. The water was about 1½ foot from the roof. And so the other guys started hollering, and I said, 'Come on guys, that's the only chance that you've got.' They came and everyone made it."

(Narrated by Leonard Santella)

THE COKE BURNER — AN ACCOUNT

by Bobby Holpit Salitrik

"The night shift must have spent their watch in the shanty keepin' warm," thought John, "too many sleepers on the upper yard." He knew that he was going to have to work fast to get the beehives fryin' again. Coke ovens that weren't burning full tunnel-head meant time and money. His time. The Company's money. John had been working the yard for years now. He could tell by looking across the tops of the runs of coke ovens, as he walked from the patch, which ovens would need tending first.

John let his eyes skim the ovens on the lower yard. The bottom run had been charged with coal. Four bricks high, he noticed. Four rows of brick set in place at the bottom of the oven door meant a forty-eight-hour burn — six ton of coal. Add two more rows of brick and two more ton of coal, and it meant the weekend was coming — a seventy-two-hour burn.

He watched the rhythm of the men working the scrapers. They were leveling the coal in the oven so that it would be even with the bricks already in place. Level coal meant good coke, no ash, no waste. They made maneuvering that eighteen-foot-bar look easy. The end of the bar that went into the oven had a scoop on it that looked like a spoon someone had bent backwards. The other end was fitted with a crosspiece. A leveling bar was then fitted into a steel flange on either side of the oven door at the four-brick height. This bar was a guide and support for the scraper to run on. The leveler would brace the crosspiece against his hip and thrust the bar into the oven, flattening or capping the mound of coal and pushing some of the coal toward the back. Then he would pull the bar to the right, scooping and leveling the coal, and then flip the bar over and repeat the movement to the left. "It was like a waltz," John thought. "One-two-three. In-right-left. One-two-three. Like a waltz."

John watched for several minutes more. The movement was pleasing. He could hear the sound of metal against coal in his head. No time could be wasted with forty ovens per man to tend in a day's time. Movements became streamlined, efficient, economical.

John resumed his walk and assessments of the day's activities. He could see the levelers begin to set the rest of the bricks in place. Ceramic chinks made their way to John. He was closer now. Dry brick against dry brick. Chink, chink, chink, chink, chink as the door of the oven closed to within three inches of the top of the arch. Then the truck holding the mixture of soft mud and clay was pushed down the track into place. The mud was shoveled with sharp splats against the bricks. The men then

A run of coke ovens

daubed the door smooth with trowels. Joe always boasted that he held the yard record. He could, although no one had ever witnessed it, complete an oven in five minutes. John smiled to himself; he knew that it took at least twice as long. John quickened his pace, "Better get those beehives to fryin'." He shook his head, "Never could figure that one, they look more like sixteen foot igloos to me."

John crossed the yard to where the levelers were working and exchanged greetings with his friends as he filled a bucket with mud and clay. Then he headed toward the supply house to pick up the other tool of his trade, newspaper. He grabbed a stack of papers and began tearing them into strips.

Armed with what he needed to begin his work, the Coke Burner started for the sleepers he had seen in the upper yard. They were in run #1 and #2, if he remembered correctly, and he usually did. A sleeper is an oven that, for one reason or another, burns down faster than it is supposed to. It is the Coke Burner's job to keep all the ovens burning at the same rate. Ovens that burn out before the required time of the charge, whether it is a forty-eight- or seventy-two-hour charge, will not have sufficient time to burn all of the coal and convert it into coke.

John reached the upper yard and found the sleepers in runs #1 and #2. He looked into the first oven through the air space at the top of the door. The flames were coming up in intermittent tendrils, stringing he called it. He knew that if he cut some of the air going into the oven it would start up again. Reaching into his bucket, John grabbed a trowel-full of mud. With a flick of his wrist, he placed it in between the first of the three mud patches that already equally divided the arched air space. He then placed a mud patch between each of the remaining spaces. He quickly repeated the process on the other sleepers and then stood back to watch. Within five minutes all the ovens were shooting flames four feet above the hole in the top oven, called the tunnel. John looked down the run, all were burning full tunnel-head, 2,800°F, no sleepers here.

He turned to go back down to where the men were charging the ovens on the lower runs. At one o'clock he would come back up here to cut more air on the rest of the ovens as he had cut the sleepers.

The Levelers had moved far down the track when John got back to the bottom run. The ovens that had been charged first were beginning to glow red, and then wisps of smoke and flame could be seen sneaking up through the black coal. If left alone, these ovens would be burning in an hour or two, but there was a way to set them off fast.

The Coke Burner reached around to the strips of paper that he had wadded in his back pocket. He took two strips off and placed them across the air space in the top of the oven door. The paper was sucked tight against the arch and looked like the point of a triangle. John worked his way down the run placing two strips of paper on each oven. The paper cut off all the air and held the heat in. The rising temperature caused the coal to melt and bubble like molten lava. "Fryin'" John called it. After every three or four ovens, he would lean back and glance over his shoulder down the run. He could see the smoke starting. First, a thin blue smoke that gave off some of the gasses that were forming. Next came the yellow sulfur smoke. Slow at first, then thicker, heavier, it convulsed from the tunnel, changing to a dark dirty yellow. John took in short, shallow breaths of air. He didn't have to look for that smoke, he could smell it. The smoke turned darker and thicker until it was coal black and just as dense. John listened. "Should be anytime now, she's really pushin'." Then it came, a sound like a thunderous staccato burst of wind. John looked back down to the beginning of the run. He saw the first of the paper strips being shot across the yard. A split second of dead air, then clear bright red flames shot skyward, full tunnel-head. The first of the ovens had caught and already the steps were being repeated domino style down the run.

John continued working his way down the line until he came to the ladder that led to the top of the ovens. He climbed up and walked back over the ovens he had just fired. First, he looked at the row of flames. They should all be the same height. Most were, but here and there were a few that weren't quite high enough. He threw a wad of paper into these and stood back. Again the sudden updraft of an explosion, again red flames. The Coke Burner was also checking to see if any of the ovens had dampers on. The dampers were made from corrugated tin a little larger than the tunnel-head. The damper, like the strips of paper, kept the heat inside the oven to hasten ignition of the coal. The damper had to be removed when the smoke started to roll, or the coal would crust over and not melt. If the Coke Burner found an oven that had crusted, he inserted a long metal rod with a claw on the end into the tunnel-head and broke the crust.

There was a little game, like an office joke, that the Coke Burners liked to play on new men in the yard. As they were showing the new man around the yard, they would take him for a walk on top of the ovens. When they came to a damper, the Coke Burner would raise it up, throw in a piece of paper and drop the damper back down. In a few seconds that oven would shoot so hard it would blow the damper several feet into the air. Needless to say, the new man was impressed.

A vibration in the lorry tracks that John was walking on signaled that the lorries were charging the next run of ovens, and they would soon be ready for firing. The lorries were steel cars that carried the coal from the tipple to the ovens. Low-sulfur bituminous coal was deep mined on the same yard that the coke was made. The coal was hoisted from the mine and, by means of a conveyor system, stored in a coal bin inside the tipple. The lorries were then backed under the tipple, and the cars were loaded or charged with coal. One man, called the Charger, would operate two lorries at a time. The Charger knew how much coal to load by the marks in each lorry. One mark for the forty-eight hour burn, a higher mark for the seventy-two hour burn. He moved his electrically powered cars down the tracks to the waiting ovens. After lining the lorries up with the ovens the Charger would lower a chute, located on the side of the car, into the tunnel-head and charge the oven with coal. Both lorries could be emptied from the same position on the track, because the spacing of the lorries equaled that of the ovens.

"Half of the day gone and half of the ovens tended," John calculated. "Well, one more than half — two hundred and fifty ovens out of four hundred and ninety-nine. Always one short of an even number." John chuckled to himself; he always did when he thought about it. "The Company was nobody's fool, not even Uncle Sam's. Build one more oven and pay tax on five hundred. Leave your count at four hundred and ninety-nine and pay tax on four hundred. Yes sir, those Company men were always thinkin'." He picked up his bucket of mud and started again for the upper yard. The air had to be cut on those ovens so that the

Opening the coke oven

Machine Man could pull the coke at four o'clock the next morning.

There was only one shift on the coke yard, but the starting times were staggered. Six-man crews were assigned to tend each run of ovens. A run was usually between forty and fifty ovens. There were two Levelers, they came on at six; one Charger, he came on at seven; one Water Boy, he came at two in the morning; one Machine Man, he came on at four in the morning; and one Scraper, he also came to work at four. Four stone masons took care of repairing the area inside the ovens (called the crown) when they became damaged. Stone masons began work at seven in the morning. Two Coke Burners tended the entire yard. These two men were the only ones to work at night. They would rotate shifts; one Coke Burner

Watering the coke

was on the yard at all times. With all the ovens to tend, the half that was burning and the half that was being charged and all that distance to cover, twice each shift, the Coke Burner didn't have much time to waste.

Again John made his rounds of the upper yard to make the second cut. He looked into the first oven and everything in there was almost white. He could see the heat. It made the little strings of flame look like they were dancing.

When an oven is first fully ignited, it will burn close to twenty-four hours without any attendance. As the twenty-four hour mark approaches, the ovens begin to die back. Then, they are cut the first time; at this time, the air draft is reduced by covering the vent with three mud

Coke burner

patches. The temperature of the oven rises again; the vent is made smaller, forcing the air even closer to the crown. The ovens again burn full tunnel-head for about the next ten hours, and again die back and are cut a second time. The flame is again revived and comes full tunnel-head for another ten hours. It then dies down, and the oven begins to cool. There is nothing left to burn. Coal is now coke and waiting to be pulled.

John finished the upper runs. "There shouldn't be any problems here for the rest of the burn." He gave the ovens a final inspection. The height and uniformity of the flames told him that the ovens had been cut properly. "Well, I better start back; it's quittin' time," he thought, "and time for supper."

Coke machine ready to pull coke
(Note the pile of ashes between the machine and second set of tracks)

That night, while John was sleeping, the Water Boy would come in to prepare the coke for pulling. He would tear the doors all the way down with a bar that looked like a ten-foot allen wrench. He would open ten, maybe fifteen ovens. The sprinklers would then be set into place. The sprinkler was a long pipe with a nozzle that spun around much like that of a lawn sprinkler. The Water Boy would turn on the water and watch for the first turn of the nozzle in the oven. He had to make sure that he had the sprinkler positioned so that it would water the coke—not the crown of the oven. Water on the crown would take away the heat, making it hard to ignite the next charge. When he was sure that the sprinkler was properly placed, he would hook up the next sprinkler in tandem, again watching to see where the water fell. The Water Boy would rig four sprinklers at a time, watering the coke for fifteen minutes. While he was waiting, he would pick up the bricks from the oven doors and throw them across the set of tracks that ran in front of the ovens. The bricks had to be moved so that the Machine Man could get his rig in to pull the coke. The Water Boy continued to work down the run, tearing down the doors, moving the sprinklers, removing the bricks.

The coke machine would then roll down the set of tracks next to the ovens. Steel hoppers were moved into place on a parallel set of tracks on the other side of the machine. It was a mammoth, awkward, "galumphing" machine. The Machine Man rode in a cab that was centered over the tracks. From the side facing the ovens jutted a long arm, the ram-bar. The end of the ram-bar looked like the head of a hammerhead shark with a flap on each side. The ram-bar would push under the coke, the flaps would rise as the bar was withdrawn, and the coke was pulled out of the oven, onto a flat conveyor. The Machine Man could swing the ram-bar from side to side sweeping the width of the oven. The flat conveyor pulled the coke to a second conveyor that was inclined up to the steel hoppers. As the coke was tumbled up this incline, it passed over a screen. Ashes and other small debris would fall through the screen into a pan and be channeled back onto the coke yard. The coke would continue up the second conveyor and drop into the hoppers waiting below.

Behind the coke machine came the Scraper. John would see him finishing up when he came on tomorrow morning. It was the Scraper's job to pull the coke that the Machine Man could not pull from the very edges of the ovens. He used the same scraper that the Levelers used, the eighteen-foot bar with the bent, spoon-shaped end, but he didn't have the same rhythm. His movements were efficient, and economical, and streamlined, but the rhythm was wrong, almost discordant. Even the sound of metal against coke sounded wrong. John didn't like to hear the Scraper work. He didn't know why, maybe it was just the rhythm.

This account is based on a cokeyard in Fayette County, Pennsylvania, in the 1940s. The process of burning coke in a beehive oven is now history. The last full-scale operations of beehive ovens closed here in the early 1970s. "Beehives are all done — they don't use no more beehive coke."

(Reconstructed from the account of John W. Holpit)

HOME AND COMMUNITY

Brownfield, Pa., circa 1910

Although the following narratives illustrate that patch life was difficult and at times unpleasant, they also show that the miner and the company worked together to keep houses and yards neat, clean, and orderly; and that the neighbors in the community had a very close-knit relationship with one another.

HOUSES

LAMBERT   "At first the houses were painted all red on the upper end and all light gray on the lower side. They were painted red, brown, and green later. All of the houses were rented, and the company furnished the paint for the houses and even the labor. The floors were plain wooden floor boards, and throw rugs were made from old canvases thrown away by the mine. In the windows were dark green linen shades with crocheted curtains and a stick at the top to hold them up.

"Every other house had a twenty-four-foot ladder on the side provided by the company for repair work and patch painting. These were shared. Long ditches were on each side of the road and the company kept them clean. There were huge trees planted by the company lining each side of the road, which gave an archway effect. The company did any repair work to your house or sidewalks and even furnished a small wooden garbage bin in the back yard and had a man with a horse and wagon to collect it."

(Narrated by Ann Gamon and Mary Shuman;
retold by Patricia Romito)

"This was a nice clean patch. When superintendent Rex came here, he gave common ground on the outskirts where everyone could graze their animals and have gardens. He had men go around and clean things up. In the summertime there wasn't a weed in the company property. The company took care of the houses. They painted the houses, made boardwalks for the people, also ash boxes. They had this patch pretty nice."

(Narrated by George Badovinac)

FOOTEDALE   "The house and its facilities were very crude. A 'heat-rolla' was used to heat the living room, and the cast iron stove kept the kitchen warm. All of the rooms were furnished in a simple manner; only an old leather davenport and a single table in the living room; plain

A company house

wooden table and chairs in the kitchen; one bed in each of the bedrooms, with a trunk to store clothes. The floors were rough wood, with throw or 'spot' carpeting. Each room was lit by a single bulb hanging from a 'rag' or cloth cord. There was one sink per house, and it only had one faucet of cold water. Each double house also had a double 'outhouse.' The sewers were open, and the water from other houses above them would drain in front of their house.

"The company or mine owners took care of the houses. Every spring workmen would come and replace the picket fences, or give the family wood to repair any damage. They would also leave lime so that the family could mix it with water and paint the fence. About every third or fourth year, the houses were painted (every other one red, and those in between green). The family living in the house would also have to whitewash the interior walls unless they had some type of covering over the rough plaster. Some people used newspaper to hide the ugly walls. There were also wooden sidewalks that had to be repaired every year. After the snow melted, the streets and yards were so muddy you couldn't walk. The workmen would spread ashes over the mud, but the dirt from the ashes made everything filthy."

(Narrated by Stanley Machinsky; retold by Kimberly Collins)

Double outhouse

CONTINENTAL #1   "Living in a patch wasn't very pleasant, especially in the wintertime. In the summer, you had a garden and made a nice yard and fixed it up, and you had your vegetables fresh all the time. But the house in the wintertime was cold. All you had to heat it with was a fireplace. I'd never want a fireplace now because all I can remember is the grates we used to have in every room. You used to put a grate in on the coal and wood and that's all you had for heat. You'd stand on the front of it, and you'd get too warm while your back would be freezing. You couldn't go in the corners of the room because it would be too cold. And you had to fire up your kitchen stove — it was alright in the winter time, but in summer time it wasn't very nice to fire up a coal stove to even heat the little bit of water you had to have for your dishes and your cooking or pot of tea or coffee. You would have a porch that you could go out and sit on. Most of the houses were built on hills — that made it nice in the summer but sure did make it cold in the winter. You'd be scrubbing your kitchen floor and the first thing you knew, before you got one place wiped, the place where you just scrubbed would be frozen ice."

(Narrated by Viola Ryan)

Prize-winning flower garden

YARDS

LAMBERT   "Everyone had a vegetable or flower garden in their yard with wooden sidewalks and wooden fences. Once a year the fences were whitewashed for the Fourth of July celebration."

(Narrated by Ann Gamon and Mary Shuman;
retold by Patricia Romito)

GRINDSTONE   "Every spring, when your yard was cleaned and the flowers in bloom, the company awarded prizes for the three best gardens. There was a five dollar first prize, a three dollar second prize, and a one dollar third prize. Then you got a picture framed saying you won the prize."

(Narrated by Albert Murray; retold by Debi Sabo)

SPECIAL OCCASIONS

WEDDINGS   "For weddings at Lambert, the entrance way into the yard of the bride was decorated with crepe paper and flowers. A quartet was present to play as the bride left the house to go to the church. It consisted of an accordion, bass fiddle, saxophone, and fiddle. The bass fiddle was the favorite because anyone requesting a song usually threw money into the bass. When the married couple returned home, a piece of crepe paper was strung across the gateway with a boy and a girl baby doll attached. The new husband cut the dolls and gave the girl doll to his wife and kept the boy."

(Narrated by Ann Gamon and Mary Shuman;
retold by Patricia Romito)

FUNERALS   "When someone died in Lambert, the body was brought home for preparation and viewed there. All of the neighbors came over and stayed day and night for three days and three nights. Someone was always awake. On the fourth morning, the body was buried."

(Narrated by Ann Gamon and Mary Shuman;
retold by Patricia Romito)

"If you were my neighbor and you died, the next day the beer wagon was out there, and the whole big wagon was loaded with gallon kegs of beer, and they went on for two or three days like that—drinking, eating. They said you should cry when people come into the world and laugh when they go out."

(Narrated by Bill Burke)

GREEN SUNDAY   "Daddy always kept holidays. For example, on 'Green Sunday' [a spring celebration in May on Pentecost Sunday] all of those limbs had to be pounded on the porch. Daddy would go out in the woods and he would get a big limb or a couple limbs and he would pound them on each pole of the porch—like you put your flag up, and that was 'Green Sunday.' There were special rolls you baked for that day, and all the neighbors would visit one another."

(Narrated by Rose Duran)

Wedding custom—the bridal arch (Note the suspended dolls)

COMMUNITY SPIRIT

The people living in the coal towns of southwestern Pennsylvania demonstrated a high degree of cooperation and concern for each other. What follows are individual reflections on the social spirit which prevailed in these mining patches during the early part of the twentieth century.

"The remarkable thing about those mine patches [like Leisenring #1] was the fellowship and brotherhood that existed among the people. There was never any discrimination because of ethnic background or wealth or poverty or anything of that kind, everybody was for everybody, and it was really remarkable. A person walking down through the patch knew, not only where he was going, but what he was thinking. And maybe it was a good thing from the moral standpoint because everybody had to be cautious and careful, not necessarily because they were that virtuous, but because they knew that every eye in the place was on them, and they had to be virtuous whether they wanted to be or not."

(Narrated by Judge James A. Reilly)

A company store

"Yes, the people [in Edenborn] were a lot friendlier. If you were in want for anything—a loaf of bread, a piece of bread, you know they'd give it to you. I can tell you that there was nobody in want. Anybody got sick, your neighbors came in to see if you wanted something, colored people, white people, made no difference what religion you were or anything. Oh, these times ain't like them. No sir, people ain't like they used to be."

(Narrated by John Coll)

"When we lived in Lambert, old Mr. Rex was superintendent. When Fourth of July come, we used to have good times. There were fireworks, games (three-legged races), and everything. Lambert was a good patch at that time — good, clean, nice — just like here [Filbert]. Everybody worked well together and helped each other."

(Narrated by Anthony Kazmierczak)

Interior of a company store

THE COMPANY STORE

In each patch, one building stood out among all others; it was the company store. This store provided all the essentials of life for the miner and his family: food, clothes, gas, mail, gifts, and hardware. In addition, it served as the miner's place of wage payment and often as a meeting or recreation hall. The relationship between the company store and the mining community was sometimes good and sometimes bad, as illustrated by the following narratives.

"Each mining patch had a company store where a miner had to do all of his shopping, and the company expected you to spend all of your earnings at the store. Like in the song, you owed your soul to it because you had to spend all your earnings at the store or you would lose your job."

(Narrated by Mike Gugar)

"All of your shopping had to be done in the company store. If the mine superintendent found out that you weren't [shopping there], he would give you less work or else harder jobs. The company store carried everything needed by the families, including meat, dry goods, and clothes. Whenever you purchased something, the clerk added it to your bill. Your bill was then deducted from your pay check. The miners knew that they would never 'get ahead' of the company store."

(Narrated by Stanley Machinsky; retold by Kimberly Collins)

"I wouldn't buy from the company store. What was three dollars in the company store was one dollar in town."

(Narrated by John Petrisko)

"You had to buy so much stuff from the company store, and they would send out girls to get the orders, and you had to give them an order every week. The girl who worked at the company store would come to your house and get an order of flour or whatever you needed, and then they would deliver it to you. But you had to buy there. You didn't pay when they delivered — they took it out of your pay. If you didn't buy at the company store, they wouldn't want you to work in the mine then. You had to spend so much there. It was cheaper in the other stores than it was in the company store. I bought some groceries at other stores — the company didn't mind—but you had to give them an order, some kind of an order, every week.

(Narrated by Anna Billek)

"A company store was a variety store like Gee Bees. But it wasn't that big. It was a grocery, clothing, hardware, and gift store all in one. It was also the post office and gas station for the patch. It was two stories tall. The food was sold on the first floor and the miscellaneous items on the second floor. Very few people could go to a large town to shop; so they had to buy everything they needed at the company store. Most mothers would make dresses or shirts for their children from the material sold at the company store. Some girls were lucky enough to get a ready-made dress, but they sometime had the same dress other girls got. Occasionally, people used the company store as a meeting place."

(Narrated by Johanna Swetz)

"With the company store, no one needed to leave the patch. It carried everything necessary to live, and even had gas pumps and only the best quality merchandise. The only thing missing was church."

(Narrated by Ann Gamon and Mary Shuman;
retold by Patricia Romito)

"Mr. Hughes came there as the store boss and he wanted to do good by everybody. He came around to each and every family and would give you tickets for every person that was in your family, even the adults got the tickets for it, and this was to give you candy at Christmas time. And then, about two or three days before Christmas, he closed the store and everybody would congregate there, and they'd all sing Christmas carols."

(Narrated by Tekla Hensh Skomra)

"Oh, yeah, the company store was good to me—it was a very good store. They were like all the rest of the stores—they all treated me good. If I wanted to buy something at the company store, I'd have to go back to the cashier and say, I want to draw a ten dollar check. She'd give me a check that would be worth ten dollars. I could use that check up until the ten dollars was out. After I spent that ten dollars, I'd draw another one. Then when payday came, they would have it all deducted out, and you would get all your change in an envelope."

(Narrated by Bill Burke)

"The worst time was during the depression, but the company store did see that you had a little bit of something to eat. They would give you so much. And it was really better than what a lot of people think it was. They talk about the store not being good to you, but it was; it seemed that any time miners were out of work, or there was sickness in the family, the company store would carry you over and give you anything you had to have."

(Narrated by Viola Ryan)

"I had no trouble with the company store. They were a little dear, but they had good stuff. I never bought and got in debt with them. I tried to stay within my earnings. Some people misused the company stores — they bought more than they ever earned and they condemned the stores. But

I had no fault with the company store. They trusted people to the point where they owed too much, and they had to cut them off. But I never had any trouble."

(Narrated by an anonymous miner; retold by Daryl Walker)

"More coal was loaded on the company store porch [during bull sessions] than in the mines."

(Narrated by Harold Seaton)

RECREATION

Baseball

According to Stanley Machinsky, a resident of the Footedale and Buffington patches, "baseball was the biggest form of recreation in the mining towns. Every patch in this area had its own team." For the people in the summer, "watching the games was the highlight of the week and the people walked for miles, sometimes up to eight miles one way, to see their team." Bill Burke, an all around player and manager for the Lambert team, remembers that "baseball was it," the main activity in a mining town. As a player, he sometimes played "six to eight games a week."

Alex Whoolery, a Fayette County Hall of Famer, recalls how he played his way through three different leagues in the Oliphant and Grays Landing patches during the early 1920s and later. As a small boy, he played on an "informally organized" team of nine- to thirteen-year-olds who had no adult supervision. An older boy was chosen "keeper of the team," and he would arrange all the games. Unlike little leaguers today, the boys of the patch had no adult interference. They "organized and disciplined themselves."

After playing on the youth team, Alex made "the second nine," a team having players usually between the ages of fourteen and eighteen. Afterwards, he was selected to "the first nine." Members of this team were considered to be "the real pros" and "the big men of the patch, idolized by all the kids."

Alex recalls that "baseballs were hard to come by" in his day. For example, in the youth league, the boys played with "home-made taped balls." To make a baseball, "the boys took a rubber ball, wrapped string around it, and then covered it with black tape donated by an electrician or mechanic."

Sometimes the boys would acquire a regulation ball by going to see

Hall of Famer Alex Whoolery

"the first nine" play. On a foul tip, "they would chase the ball, stomp it down into the ground, mark the spot, and return later to claim the ball."

Another scarce piece of equipment was a ball glove. Alex recalls that "he did not have a glove until after he was married." Then he had one because he played first base for "the first nine." On the youth team, or second nine, only two players regularly had gloves — the first baseman and the catcher. The others used "bare hands or old, discarded leather work gloves from the mine."

In the early 1920s, transportation to an away game was by foot. Traveling often took three hours one way. Usually, lunches were not packed. On the way, Alex and others would stop "to eat wild berries, apples, peaches, or ripe, raw corn."

For the purpose of raising money, Alex remembers, "patch festivals — with their special treats of ice cream — and dances were often planned around an important home game." Before the game, the patch band would parade through the streets to arouse interest and then lead everyone to the game. After playing at the game, the band would march players and fans to the festival area and pavillion, where a dance would normally end the festivities.

"A good ballplayer," says Alex, "did not have a difficult time getting a job." In fact, some companies tried to steal good players from other companies by offering them better jobs and more money. In addition, some players received "special treatment at work." They were permitted to "take it easy by lying down in the hay at the stable during the morning." And then, at lunch time, they left the mine to practice for the game. Alex and others rejected such treatment. They found satisfaction and honor in doing a full, hard day's work.

Baseball was important in the patch, says Stan Machinsky, because it "served a dual purpose. The company encouraged the games because baseball was a good way for the miners to relieve their frustrations from the living conditions or the work. And the miners enjoyed the activity."

Children's Games

During the evenings, Sunday afternoons, and summer days, children of the patch could be seen and heard playing games, such as socky, caddy, shinny, lay-low sheepy, and hoops. Descriptions of these games and other forms of recreation were reconstructed from the recollections of Mary Shuman, Ann Gamon, and Patricia Romito, who lived in Lambert patch; Carmen Guappone, who lived in Puritan; Andrew Duran, who lived in Allison #2 and Royal; and Rose Duran, who lived in Allison #2, Royal, Phillips, and Leith.

SOCKY BALL   This game was played with a round ball made from a pair of old, worn socks, "originally the brown cotton socks women wore in the 1900s." Directions for making a socky ball are: "Place one sock inside the other; then hit it against a hard surface to pack it down. Twist the top of the sock and turn it inside out over top of the ball and hit again to pack. Continue until all of the outer sock is wrapped over the ball; then stitch opening closed."

Any number of children could play the game. Only two players batted at one time; the rest were in the field. In addition to home plate, there was only one other base. A pitcher would toss the socky underhand, and a batter would hit the ball with his open or closed hand. To get the batter out, a fielder would try to hit him with the ball while he was running to the base or back to home. As soon as any fielder recorded an out, he would get a turn at bat. His position in the field would be taken by the batter who was hit by the socky. The game would continue in this pattern indefinitely.

CADDY   This game had two pieces of equipment — a caddy and a caddy stick. A caddy was "a four-inch piece of square wood whittled on both ends to a point." On one side of the caddy "an X was burned with a poker from the stove." On the second side, one notch was made; on the third side, two notches; and on the fourth side, three notches. These notches indicated the number of turns a player had to hit the caddy. A caddy stick was "a flat stick approximately two feet long," with one end carved as a handle to fit one's grip.

To begin the game, the players made a goal line "at a distance of about one hundred yards." Then each player rolled the caddy to see how many turns he had to get the caddy across the goal. The maximum number of turns was three. If the caddy turned up an X, the player was out of the game.

With the caddy stick, a player hit the caddy on one of its pointed ends. When the caddy flew into the air, the player hit it as hard as he could toward the goal line. If the caddy landed in a ditch, puddle, or bush, the player had to play the caddy from that position. He could not move it. The first one across the goal was the winner.

SHINNY   The format of this game was simple. Two holes were dug at opposite ends of a field. There were no boundaries. The object of the game was to get a point by hitting a used Carnation milk can into the opponent's hole in the ground. To try to do so, each player used a broomstick club. The game was "a wild, furious, physical one." The free-swinging players often hit and bruised one another on the shins and elsewhere with the broomstick clubs.

LAY-LOW SHEEPY   This game required two or more children on a side. The captain of one side would take his team members and hide them together in some part of the patch. He would then return to home base and draw in the dirt a map of the route to the hiding place. However, to confuse the opposing team, he would not indicate on the map what was north, south, east, or west. The opposing team then began to search the patch for those who were hidden. To warn those in hiding, the captain used some kind of code words, such as "apples and bananas — one meaning they are far away, the other meaning they are coming close, so lay-low sheepy." If the seekers wandered far enough away from those hiding, the latter could "sneak into home and rub out the map." They would then be the winners, and could hide again.

HOOPS   To make this toy, a child would "knock out the spokes from some old buggy or wagon wheel." He would then find a piece of firm wire. One end of the wire would be bent into a U-shape; the other end was made into a handle. Using the U-shaped part of the wire as a guide, the child would race through the streets pushing the wheel in front of him in figure-eights and other intricate patterns.

The most treasured type of hoop was made from the metal band or strip around the middle of a barrel. Children of the patch spent considerable time searching the streets and yards for the scarce center rings of barrels. These rings were in demand because they rolled the best and the straightest.

ASH DUMP PLAYGROUND   An unofficial play area for children was sometimes the ash dump at the coke yard. One of the favorite activities was to slide down the ash dump on cardboard boxes or pieces of tin that became "summertime toboggans." At night the ash dumps were popular places to play because they were adequately lit by the red glow of the nearby burning coke ovens while other parts of the patch were without light.

SWIMMING   Although some patches, like Allison #2 and Leisenring #1, had swimming pools built by the company, the children often

Community swimming pool

preferred their private, but unauthorized, swimming places in the woods or in the community reservoir which provided water for the homes and coke ovens.

MEDICINE

In the early part of the twentieth century in the coal-mining towns of southwestern Pennsylvania, there was a shortage of doctors, a shortage much greater than the one we face today. Most of the early miners and their families seldom saw a doctor. This is not to say that there was no health care in the mining patches. Usually a midwife was available to handle births. One of the older, more respected women of the community, she also sometimes handled minor crises such as lesser mine injuries. Often, a company doctor was available, but he was usually very busy and was called upon only in very serious matters. For most of the common illnesses or problems, there were home remedies.

In the mine itself, there were remedies for complaints suffered by the miners. For heartburn a miner could eat some chalk. But if a miner wanted to practice preventive medicine, he might just stay away from eating a banana in the mine. It is reported that eating bananas in the mine often caused heartburn. Another in-mine remedy—sucking on a piece of coal—was used to dissipate a bad stomach or heartburn. Apparently, this remedy is still practiced by some of the younger miners. If a shotfirer developed a headache while in the mine, it is reported that all he needed to dispel it was a touch of dynamite powder under the tongue. Or if he wanted to prevent the headache, he had to be sure not to touch his forehead with his dynamite tainted hands. It was also suggested that the plague of miners—a backache—could be treated by applying a leech to the painful area of the back.

On the home front, a variety of remedies were used. Colds apparently caused the most problems because there seem to be more remedies for that ailment than for anything else. A few examples of these include drinking a mixture of hot tea, lemon, honey, and whiskey, or a mixture of heated wine with honey. The honey was to help the cough; the heat, to dispel the cold. Other remedies for a cough included drinking warm wine plus swallowing a helping of melted Vick's salve, or drinking a mixture of carbon oil and sugar. A rather elaborate cough syrup was prepared according to the following recipe.

> "Take one, whole, fresh onion and chop it into very small pieces. Place the chopped onion into a small pot and add two cups of water and one-half cup of sugar. Cook this mixture to about one-half of its original amount (or about one-half-hour), at which time the onion pieces will be soft in texture and transparent in appearance. Use the syrup as needed to relieve coughs and sore throats."

Garlic was a favored item in the treatment of colds and flu. The cold sufferer was encouraged to take some milk and garlic and boil them together and then drink the concoction while warm. Or if one preferred, he could either eat a lot of garlic or wear a garlic necklace to prevent a cold or flu. If the cold was accompanied by aches and pains, then a mustard plaster was prepared in this way.

> "Melt two tablespoons of lard in a large skillet. To this melted lard add two or three cups of regular bread flour and a heaping teaspoon of dry mustard. Heat these ingredients on a low heat until the mixture becomes quite hot to the touch. Be certain to stir the mixture during the heating process to avoid scorching it. Pour the dry, heated mixture onto a white cloth about eighteen by eighteen inches and fold the cloth to

form a poultice. This can be applied directly to the area of the body requiring heat. It can be used to loosen the dry cough of chest colds or for the relief of muscular aches and pains."

Whooping cough was yet another winter ailment that was treated with home remedies. Parents were told to take the kids to a pitmouth (if one was nearby) and let them breathe the sulfury mine air; or if a pitmouth was not available, then a horse or a mule might be helpful. It is reported that having a horse or mule breathe on the baby or child would also help to relieve the discomforts of whooping cough.

Two remedies were suggested for an upset stomach: Either eat chicken soup or drink a mixture of baking soda, warm water, and vinegar.

In summer, when people were active, cuts and scratches abounded. To treat those, it was suggested that one should clean the wound with soap and water, wrap it in a large green leaf called "bupkovaliski," and put a little lard on the leaf. One remedy suggested using turpentine as a cleaning agent for a cut. If the cut became infected, a bread and milk poultice or raw bacon and sugar were applied to the infected area. If poison ivy was a bother, a bath in warm water and large quantities of Octagon soap were prescribed.

Another summer complaint was diarrhea. Relief was gotten sometimes with the following remedy.

"Place two tablespoons of barley in a pot. Fill this with enough water to just cover the barley. Boil this mixture for five minutes and remove it from the heat. Drain off the water. Take the boiled barley and put it into two quarts of water. Boil this mixture down to one quart. Drain off the remaining quart of liquid and take it in small doses as needed for relief."

A few miscellaneous items were also helpful for home health care. For a headache, a miner's wife might take a large potato and cut it into medium sized slices. She would then put these in a clean rag and wrap them around the forehead. When the potatoes turned black, the headache would be gone. Or if one was troubled with chapped hands, he rubbed them with generous amounts of lard. For an earache, some blew cigar or pipe smoke into the ear. Finally, if a person was having tooth trouble, he had only to hook a strong string to the bothersome tooth, attach the other end of the string to a door, and then get someone to open the door with a quick, strong pull. If he preferred to save the tooth for a while, he might have gotten relief from the ache in it by applying vanilla extract to it.

Apparently, patent medicines also played a part in home medical care. Many people mentioned the use of Vick's salve, Cloverleaf salve, liniments of various types (used to treat backaches), and Doan's pills (also for backaches).

This list, by no means complete, only samples the ingenuity of a people who had to be self-sufficient even in their illnesses. Home remedies were contributed by Asa Herring, Andrew Hovanec, Charles Hudek, Mary Hunchuck, Mary Margaret Malesky, Eleanor Rerko, Joseph Rerko, Nellie Schuessler, Louis Skomra, Tekla Hensh Skomra, Ann Vrobel, and Paul Vrobel.

FOODWAYS

There are probably more differences than likenesses in the foodways of the various groups that have come to be known as the bituminous miners of southwestern Pennsylvania. It is perhaps in the foodways that ethnic backgrounds have the greatest influence. When the various groups (Welsh, Scotch, Irish, English, German, Slavic, Italian, Blacks, etc.) came together in southwestern Pennsylvania and became miners, they didn't start eating "miner's food," but rather they kept on eating the foods of their original homelands. And as time went on, they assimilated the foods of the other groups into their own foodways. This assimilated diet, then, has become the food of their present-day descendants. It is not at all unusual to find a mining family of Polish or Slovak descent eating pizza or spaghetti. Nor is it unusual to find a mining family of Italian extraction eating perohi or holupki. And it is not unusual to find any family — whatever its background — savoring the venison steaks or wild rabbit stews that the earlier inhabitants of this area have always savored.

Out of this variety, however, a few lines can be drawn, and a few broad statements can be made. There are the eating habits and foodways of the miners within the mine itself, and the eating habits and foodways practiced by miners' families within the community.

As far as can be determined, most miners of the earlier half of the twentieth century carried their lunches in an oval or round two-part bucket made of aluminum or some metal alloy. The bucket had a lower container to carry the liquid, an upper container to carry the solid foods, and a lid to cover the contents. The bucket had a large handle and a lid ring, both of which were also made of aluminum or an alloy. In the bottom half of this bucket, the men carried a liquid—water, tea, or coffee.

A miner's lunch bucket

At this point, the similarities end; for each miner had his own unique lunch foods. Some carried the traditional three or four sandwiches, a fruit (apple, pear, peach, etc.), or some sort of cake or pastry. Others, particularly the Slavic miners, did not carry sandwiches but instead simply carried thick slices of homemade bread and accompanying thick slices of fried or raw bacon or ham or pork or other meat. And still other miners, those from the mountain or outlying areas, often carried some sort of roasted or fried wild meat — rabbit, squirrel, or whatever was available. There were even those who carried only a drink and slices of bread covered with thick molasses.

When were these lunch foods eaten? Once again it seems that there was no regular practice. The miners ate when they found the time and wherever they found a place. They sat on a rail or a lump of coal or on the ground. Usually, they ate in their work places, although some mines did have a dinner hole or an area that was set off for eating purposes. Also, they often ate alone although sometimes they did not. Some men had a habit of eating with a buddy or some other men in the area on a regular basis. Cleanliness was a difficult habit to maintain in the mines, and so they ate with dirty hands and faces. If they wore gloves, however, they were lucky. They had clean hands and clean bread.

Two other items should be mentioned about the in-mine eating habits. First, it seems that some mines were subject to a good deal of thieving.

Food just seemed to disappear. No one was ever sure of whether the thief was human or animal. Although most believed the thief to be human, some blamed the ever present mine rat for the disappearing foods. Some, rather than worrying about whom to blame, simply decided to outsmart the thief by eating their lunches as soon as they got to their work places. Second, if any part of the lunch was left (either by chance or design) at the end of the day, two groups of beings enjoyed the treat. Some miners would throw morsels of their food to the begging mine rats. Others saved half of a sandwich or a slice of meat and took it home to the kids. Many miners' children thought the food that had sat in the mine air all day had a particularly unique flavor and looked forward to their father's return with his small treat.

At home a variety of foods and customs of eating flourished. Each family retained its ethnic diet and customs. Those of northwestern European backgrounds enjoyed roasts, beef stews, potatoes, puddings, and jellies. Those of eastern European lineage ate soup (which came in many varieties), bread, doughy foods, and meat (often pork). The southern Europeans had spaghetti and tomato-flavored foods, salads, and spicy meats such as salami. Others, such as the Blacks, ate green leafy vegetables, or still others ate the wild meats of the area.

Most mining families ate dinner when the father returned home from work at 4 p.m. or 5 p.m. or before he went to work around 3 p.m. or 4 p.m. Of course, this time changed when the shifts changed, or when the miner found it necessary to work longer hours. Generally, the family ate as a family if at all possible. Sundays, in particular, were the time for a big family meal with special foods. In some families, the mother spent most of her time hovering around the table rather than sitting at the table. She was not only the cook, but also the waitress, the busgirl, and the dishwasher, unless she had older girls to help her. Leftovers were never thrown away; they were saved for future use or fed to the family animals. Little if anything was wasted.

Foods were obtained in several ways, and these were relatively standard in mining families. Certain basic items such as flour, salt, coffee, tea, sugar, etc., were bought at the company store. Bread was made once or twice a week at home and sometimes in outdoor ovens. Vegetables were raised in the family garden. This garden was often a summer-long family project. The competition for the best garden was fierce. Each gardener tried to outdo the other for the biggest cucumber or tomato. The companies, by the way, encouraged this and even provided money prizes and certificates for the best gardens. At the end of the season, the vegetables were stored by canning, drying, or burying in root cellars. In addition to caring for the garden during the summer, the children of a mining family

Prize-winning vegetable garden

spent a great deal of time scouring the countryside for berries (dewberries, blackberries, huckleberries, elderberries), wild fruits (crabapples, apples, pears), and mushrooms. These too were canned or dried. Meats were provided in three ways. Some bought their meats, but many others either raised and butchered their own hogs, cows or chickens, or hunted for deer, rabbits, and pheasants. These meats were dressed at home, and they were then eaten or preserved by salting, smoking, or canning.

Ways of preserving or preparing foods and special recipes were found in nearly all mining families. A few samples of these are recounted below.

SAUERKRAUT
"We always made a fifty-gallon barrel of sauerkraut. My dad would get a mountain of cabbage heads late in the fall. . . . Well, he'd get the cabbage and cut it up on our cabbage shredder. Then he would say, 'Annie has the long legs; Toni is too short. When Toni gets into the barrel you can't see her head, and Mary won't do it.' So I'd sit there and wash my feet and wash my feet in many waters. I washed them over and over and then sat there with my feet in salt water. They'd fill the barrel full of cabbage. Then they'd put a chair next to the barrel, and I'd step on the chair and into the barrel. And I jumped around and around and tramped the cabbage down. Then they'd lift me out and put me back in the salt water. This

continued until the barrel was filled. . . . Then they'd put the barrel in the storehouse out back, and the kraut would ferment, and they'd clean the brine off. By then the apples were in season, and we picked them and put them on top of the kraut. Then a big rock was put on top of it all, and it was covered with a clean cloth. It was ready to eat, and you could smell it a mile off."

(Narrated by Ann Vrobel)

DANDELIONS

"We'd pick dandelions and wash them in several waters and in cold water. Then we'd fry bacon in little pieces and real crisp. Then we'd throw the fat off and add some vinegar and flour to the bacon and stir in salt and pepper. Then we'd pour that gravy over the dandelions. You can prepare sauerkraut much the same way."

(Narrated by Nellie Schuessler)

WINE

"We used to go out and pick berries for maybe two or three days. We'd get a washtub full of blackberries. Everybody would go out and pick berries. Then we'd bring them home and stick them in a wooden barrel and leave them ferment. Maybe we'd add a little bit of sugar. We never put in any yeast. We'd let it ferment, and then Dad would take off the top. When the berries would raise up, he'd push them back in and take them in his hands and start crushing them. Then he would leave them there for a day or two more, and as soon as they would raise he would take a feed or flour sack and pour this heavy stuff into it and squeeze the juice out of it into this one barrel. Then he would run this stuff through again and restrain it and put it into another barrel. Then he'd let it sit like that and add some sugar to it and put it into its final barrel and leave it all for three or four days. He would add more sugar to it. Then he'd leave the putty out of the bung hole until it [the wine] quit working. Then he would seal it."

(Narrated by Joseph Rerko)

CANNED SAUSAGE

"My mother [Mrs. Henry Dantzler] canned sausage patties. She would fry the sausage patties and put them in a jar and then pour the grease into the jar. Then she'd put the top on and turn the jar upside down so the

grease would be on top. When we were ready to use them, we'd just take them out of the jar and warm them."
(Narrated by Mrs. Henry Dantzler; retold by Mr. Howard Dantzler)

As these narratives emphasize, food gathering, preparation, and preservation were a family affair, and the mining families made use of the fruits of nature that surrounded them. They did not depend upon the neighborhood supermarket. They depended upon their own energies, skills, and resourcefulness.

PAMPUSKI
(PANKUSKI)

"Out of the bread recipe, the leftover dough we left it go for Pampuski; we'd made a big pan of that and sprinkle it with sugar. [To make pampuski] you get yourself a piece of dough, and you cut it in squares or however, and let it raise a little bit. And you got your hot grease in a skillet, and you take them and put them in that skillet, like the fried doughnuts. And soon as it would brown on one side you turned it over on the other. Then you'd put them in a great big bowl. Oh, a heaping bowl and sprinkle them with sugar and have them with coffee. And, oh, that was really good. You eat four, five, six of them. We made them when we made bread, and we made bread out of 25 pounds of flour in the wooden tub."
(Narrated by Rose Duran)

KOLBASSI
(KIELBASA)

"[When we butchered the hog we'd make many things.] To make kolbassi we'd cut all that pork up in little cubes. Daddy never ground it. So we had to sit there for days, for two days or more, and cut that meat. We'd put salt and pepper and garlic and that would have to soak for two days in that wooden bucket. First, we used to clean our own casing [the intestines]. That was such a dirty mess. Well, Daddy got more modern, and he would go to the little meat market on Peter Street to get them. We had to make this into a sausage and he'd be so particular. They [the sausage-like kolbassi] had to be a certain size and so firm. Then we'd cut them [the stuffed casings] and tie them and put them on a broomstick. When it came time, when they were all ready, Daddy had a barrel out in the yard, and he dug a trench, and he put them in. Then he got the wood, and he put the wood in the fire. They couldn't be smoked too hard or they would burst. You had to do it slowly. After they got brown and smoked, Daddy would take them out. They were hung on sticks in the barrel, and the kolbassi hung down in the barrel over the fire, and the smoke came up and smoked them. Mostly Dad took care of these when he came home from work, and he knew just how to do them. Then he would smoke the hams this way too. He would put a little beef in the kolbassi too."

(Narrated by Rose Duran)

BELIEFS AND CUSTOMS

BELIEFS

Any group of people who share a common life experience tend to develop certain beliefs about life. When the life experience is filled with a good deal of the unknown and unexpected, people are forced to rely not only on reason and rational explanation but also upon intuition and the acceptance of what is not known. Some of the beliefs recorded here are still held by some people. Others are only remembered.

Some miners believed that it was bad luck to have an alarm clock fall from a mantle. If this happened, the miner would not go to work for one day.

Miners like to eat in the same spot every day with the same friends or ride in the same seat every day [in the mantrip]. When this cannot be so, some miners feel uneasy.

A woman in the mine could mean bad luck.

Some old-timers will not reenter their homes after starting their journey to the pit. It could bring ill luck.

Too much washing of the back can weaken it.

It is not a good practice to start a new job on Friday. A miner should always wait until Monday.

Some miners would not go to work if they happened to put their shirts on inside-out.

If a miner's headlight should go out or go dim, this could mean that his wife or girl friend is cheating on him.

Hanging falls in the gob area of a mine tend to fall around midnight because the earth is upside down.

Sometimes, if a woman crossed a miner's path while he was on his way to work, he would go home and miss work that day.

If a miner left for work and returned home for something he had forgotten, his wife would not permit him to enter the house. She would get whatever it was he had forgotten.

These beliefs were collected during class discussions with students enrolled in the associate degree program in mining technology at the Fayette Campus. We'd like to thank Charles Billy, Tim Deegan, Robert Hall, Michael Hauncher, Walter Kopec, Andrew Poremba, Charles Schiffbauer, John Showman, and Kenneth Turner.

CUSTOMS

Strikes and Water

The act was very simple — a miner would spill the water from the lower half of his lunch pail onto the ground. This was done in anger, frustration, resentment, despair, or (in rare cases) joy. The cause of his emotional state could have been a dispute over a specific job assignment given to him that day, company pressure for increased production, questions over mine safety, or a combination of additional personal and occupational factors. Usually the practice was premeditated; however, there were instances when it was done accidentally. Regardless of his motivation or intentions, the result of this simple, direct act was the same — a strike. This act is one which is indisputably indigenous to the mining culture and embodies elements which are both symbolic and real.

Symbolically, water has always carried spiritual and essential meanings which are profound to all mankind. Spiritually, water is used in a variety of baptism rites (total immersion to sprinkling of water on the forehead), a multitude of religious blessings (homes, fields, ships, cars, etc.), and many primitive rituals (rain dances or prayers to water spirits). Water is often associated with man's earliest beginnings. Also, each of us is

Lasting tribute to a miner

carried by our mother encased in the fluids of her womb. Finally, water is the third element in the triad of earth, fire, and water which man has viewed for ages as basic to our existence.

Realistically, water is necessary to sustain life. Louis Skomra, a retired coal miner, comments on this aspect. "There was no water in the mines years ago, no drinkable water. The water you brought from home was all that you had, and once you threw it out, you had to leave. I don't say you couldn't possibly go eight hours without drinking water, but it's not very likely. So once you threw this out, that was it! You had nothing to go on, and even if the other men wanted to go to work, you didn't go because you didn't have any water."

Culturally, the practice of throwing out their drinking water as a prelude to a strike can be viewed as a unique blend of desecration and destruction. On the one hand, the spilling was a symbolic defilement of this quasi-religious element; while on the other hand, it realistically became an act of possible self-destruction, since without the water they might perish. This traditional practice was a harbinger of many strikes in the coal fields of southwestern Pennsylvania.

Pine Tree Custom

At the Lambert Mine, R. V. Rex, the superintendent, initiated the custom in 1920 of planting pine trees in honor of those who died in the mine. These evergreens were located approximately fifty feet between the lamp house and the mine. In all, thirteen pine trees were planted in memory of men who were killed.

After the mine closed, children cut down all but one of the trees for use at Christmas time. Today, only the tree planted first is still standing. That tree, rising to a height of thirty feet or more, is a memorial to the first man killed in Lambert Mine—Paul Kochis, Sr., who died as a result of a fall on May 31, 1920.

(Reconstructed from the account of Bill Burke)

A TOUCH OF HUMOR

Pre-game shennanigans

At work, at home, and in the community, miners and their relatives, despite the hardships of their lives and the dangers of the mines, had an irrepressible sense of humor, as illustrated by the tricks and pranks recounted in the following stories.

"Before the bathhouses were put in the mine, the men would have to come home. We would put a big tub in the middle of the floor and made sure we had lots of water, and they would kneel down by the tub and we'd have to wash their backs. Of course, they would wash their face and hands and their bellies, but when it came to the back, we had to wash their backs. But while women were washing the men's backs, lots of times the women pulled tricks on the men. They'd take a little bit of water and pour it down the other end instead of down toward the head—and boy —did you ever see somebody jump!"

(Narrated by Mary Hunchuck)

Sometimes a first baseman on a patch team had a concealed peeled potato in his shirt. After an attempted pick-off play at first, the first baseman would throw the potato instead of the baseball back to the pitcher. Then, when the unsuspecting base-runner would take his next lead-off, the first baseman would tag him out with the real baseball.

(Reconstructed from an account of Alex Whoolery)

"My aunt (mother's sister) brought my mother over from Czechoslovakia to Elm Grove. So my mother come to this country—to Connellsville train station, where there was nobody to meet her. But yet there were two men there that were boarders at my aunt's house, and they were going to have some fun with my mother, thinking she was a greenhorn. ... So these guys, taking my mother to where she was suppose to go... come past the coke oven.... Mother wanted to know what's the big fire, why is that big fire there? Well, these guys say to mother, well, it is just this way — the women that come from old country have to take broom and sweep that fire out of each and every oven. My mother says, how in the world was she going to sweep fire out of oven? She comes to my aunt's house worried about how she was going to sweep that fire out. But finally they owned up to the truth. They all got a big kick out of it, but my mother didn't think it was funny."

(Narrated by Mary Hunchuck)

"I was always an ornery bugger; I said to Bill, let's play a joke on Ben, he's a big guy. I seen him coming, you know, and we had what you called a first aid canister in the mine where they kept the blankets and stretchers and the splints and stuff. I said, let's pull a fast one on him. So we both crawled in that hole there, and we wrapped ourselves around them nice blankets, and we went — whooo, whooo — and he'd go a little bit, and he'd stop, then we would wait awhile, then we would go — whooo, whooo — then he would go again. Finally, he couldn't go no more. He turned around and I bet he tore a half dozen rollers out of the middle of the track running out of the mine. He said Gussy came back to life up there. Here it wasn't Gussy at all. My dad gave me and Bill hell. He said what did you do that for? I said, well, let's get the fear out of them. I said that dead man isn't coming back no more."

(Narrated by Bill Burke)

"During my first week in the mine, I was sent to work with an old fellow, Dominick. I worked with him and all the time he hit the coal—coal fall. All the time I hit the coal—no! All the time he hit the coal, he had a habit to do like a sneeze. He would hit the coal and make a sneeze sound, and coal would fall. I hit the coal and my coal no want to come. And I say, Uncle Dominick, why you sneeze and do like that and your coal fall, and mine no want to fall? He says — you don't know how to do it [sneeze]."

(Narrated by Mike Guappone)

"Some miners are very bad about stealing each other's lunch. It gets to be a game or contest. You find them doing all kinds of things. I knew of one case where a fella was having his lunch eaten everyday; so he caught a rat and took it home and cooked it and put it in his lunch, and someone stole it and ate it. Just like they normally did. They thought it was a squirrel, evidently. And another case — a fella made a sandwich out of grease. We had a grease that looked like strawberry jam. It was real bright red in color, and it looked pretty tasty. And one fella made a sandwich out of it, and another fella stole it and ate it. And there were several cases where people would put X-Lax on cakes . . . and people would steal them and eat them."

(Narrated by Bennie Morgan)

"Well, the funniest story I ever heard was one my uncle was telling me. He worked over at Amend here. They had this fellow come in the mine.

Anyway, he got a job laying track. He got along pretty well with tracks. Then he brought his boy in, and they were supposed to put in this switch to get to another working place. They checked everything out, and then they went and shoveled out everything to be ready to start laying the track. So they brought the rails and everything in. They were supposed to have a frog [a metal device with four protruding prongs used to transfer a coal car from the main track to an intersection or side track]. In the meantime, as they walked in and out of the place they had to step around this big puddle of water. Anyway, the father told the boy, 'Okay, I'll start working in here, but you go down to the main track and get a frog.' So the young kid went down to the track, and he sat there and sat there and waited and waited. Pretty soon his daddy came up and said, 'Hey, did you get that frog?' The kid looked up and said, 'Pap, he hasn't come up yet.' After that they called that kid Froggy."

(Narrated by Joe Rerko)

"Dony Sweeney [Dominick] was a good ballplayer with me in Leisenring in my time. He was a very good outfielder but a weak batter. Dony was a tough guy — he could take a hit. So, many times he would turn his side around, and take a hit in the ribs and thus got on base. Of course, his mother, Mrs. Sweeney, was very proud of her Dony, even though she didn't know much about the game. She would go around bragging to everyone who would listen, telling what a great player her Dony was. One evening she was telling about Dony's achievements on the baseball field when someone asked her what Dony played — what position he played. She said she didn't know but she thinks he was the Batter. Of course, that's the one thing that Dony wasn't — the Batter."

(Narrated by Judge James A. Reilly; retold by Margaret Reilly Skomra)

Even in the face of adversity, mining families often tried to maintain good spirits, to lighten their sorrows with a bit of humor.

"I recall the time one of the miners was caught in a fall of slate and it was a fatal accident. After many hours the miners extricated him from the fall, and he was brought to the surface. Of course, the news got about that there was a fatal accident in the mine. The ball team had just come back from a game, and they were close to the scene. There was a call for volunteers to take the dead miner up to his home in the patch. It was suggested that they wanted somebody who could be diplomatic about it and break the news to the widow.

"This one fellow spoke up and said that he could take care of the situation, and by now night was coming. So he and another ballplayer took the dead miner up to his home and knocked at the door.

"Mrs. Rafferty [fictitious] came to the window upstairs and wanted to know what they wanted. One of the men [the ballplayer charged with the burden of being discreet] said, 'Does the Widow Rafferty live here?' She replied, 'I'm Mrs. Rafferty, but I'm no widow!' The ball player answered, 'The hell you're not. Here's your Mike.'"

(Narrated by Judge James A. Reilly)

GLOSSARY

Black damp—Generally applied to carbon dioxide. It is also applied to an atmosphere that is oxygen deficient in relation to human needs.

Buddy system — Practice of having two or three men work a place together. The buddies loaded coal together, ate together, came and went together. See page 10 for further description.

Carbide lamp —Early mine light that preceded the present battery lamp. It burned the gas formed by mixing carbide with water and was lighted by using a flint. The light was mounted on the miner's cap. The mine lamp has evolved from candles to whale oil lamps and Anton lamps, to carbide lamps, to battery lamps.

Company store — General store owned and operated by a coal company. It sold just about anything and provided credit to the miners. See page 47 for further description.

Cut—Actual slice of a coal seam. The process consists of cutting a strip of coal five inches high and several feet deep into the coal at either the top or bottom of the seam. This is followed by blasting the coal out. The older miners referred to the amount of coal to be loaded from this operation as a cut. See page 13 for further description.

Fire boss —Member of the managerial ranks directly in charge of mine safety inspection, particularly with reference to gas detection. Originally, the fire boss was the man sent underground to burn out the methane gas before the rest of the men came into the mine.

Frog —Metal device with four protruding prongs used to transfer a coal car from the main track to an intersecting or side track.

Gas — Generally denotes methane gas.

Gob —That part of a mine from which the coal has been removed and the space then more or less filled. When all of the coal is removed, the mined out area caves in. When this cave-in occurs, the area is said to have fallen, and the part is then referred to as the gob.

Haulageway — Underground passageway designed for the transportation of men, materials, and coal. At one time it referred to the track area of the mine used for the movement of coal wagons. Today coal is often transported from a mine via a conveyor belt.

Machine man (cutter) — Men who operated the cutting machine. They cut a five-inch slot in the coal to provide room for allowing the coal to be broken from its seam. This process can be done by machine, but in the earlier days it was done by pick.

Manhole — Refuge hole constructed in the side of a haulageway, gangway, tunnel, or slope. It is five or more feet deep, about four feet wide, and at least four feet high. It is level with the roadway.

Mantrip — Train of mine cars used to transport men into the mine in the hand loading era. Mantrips today are either specially constructed cars pulled by a locomotive, or self-propelled personnel carriers specially constructed for transporting workmen.

Methane lamp (safety lamp) — Used to detect the presence of methane gas and oxygen deficiency. It was first used in England. Before its development miners tested for gas by burning a hemp rope. In the presence of methane, the rope would glow brighter, but it could just as easily have caused an explosion as prevent one. The present methane lamp has an enclosed flame, thus eliminating the chance of causing an explosion.

Miner's cap or hat — The miner had to place his light somewhere. They have evolved from cloth hats to soft leather hats, to hard leather hats, and then to a variety of fiber-type hard hats. A strong plastic or fiberglass hat is used today.

Patch — Name given to a mining town in most areas of Pennsylvania. This town is usually made up of rows of nearly identical single or double houses, a company store, a church, a school, and the mine.

Red dog — Non-volatile product derived from the oxidation of coal or coal refuse. It is a product of uncontrolled burning of coal or coal refuse piles. It is red in color and was used very successfully for road building and the topping of unpaved roads. If the red dog used was too fine, however, the road turned to a sea of red mud when it was exposed to freezing, thawing, spring rains, etc.

Rib — Solid coal on either side of any underground passage.

Scab — Miner who works when others are on strike. A highly derogatory name.

Shotfirer — Miner responsible for blasting the coal loose. See page 14 for further explanation.

Slack — Fine, dust-like coal. The finest sized soft coal.

Slate — Shale found with or above the coal.

Squeeze — Settling (without breaking) of the roof and the gradual rising of the floor of the mine, with the possibility of the two eventually meeting.

Stopping — Wall built to deflect or impede the flow of ventilating air in a mine.

Tail chain — Chain that attached the draft animal to the wagon.

Tipple — Hoisting super-structure at a mine when coal cars were hoisted out of the mine through a shaft. The coal came to the surface in dump cars which were then tipped over, and the load of coal was dumped into a bin. The term is no longer in use. See page 21 for a picture.

Yellow dogs — Derogatory name applied to the Iron and Coal Police of the early twentieth century. They are sometimes confused with the current State Police.
*(Reconstructed from the accounts of Willard McClain
and Bennie E. Morgan)*

SELECTED FURTHER READING

OF GENERAL INTEREST

Nonfiction

Adams, James Taylor. *Death in the Dark: A Collection of Factual Ballads of American Mine Disaster.* Big Laurel, Virginia: Adams-Mullins Press, 1941.

Brophy, John. *A Miner's Life.* Madison: University of Wisconsin Press, 1964.

Carawan, Guy and Candie. *Voices From the Mountains.* New York: Alfred A. Knopf, 1975.

Finley, Joseph E. *The Corrupt Kingdom: The Rise and Fall of the United Mine Workers.* New York: Simon and Schuster, 1972.

Humphrey, Hiram B. *Historical Summary of Coal Mine Explosions in the United States, 1810–1958.* U.S. Bureau of Mines Bulletin 586. Washington, D.C.: Government Printing Office, 1960.

Orwell, George. *The Road to Wigan Pier.* New York: Harcourt Brace, Jovanovich, Inc., 1958. (1972 paperback.)

Fiction

Critchton, Robert. *The Camerons.* New York: Warner Books, 1974.

Lillo, Baldomero. *The Devil's Pit and Other Stories.* Translated by Esther S. Dillon and Angel Flores. Washington, D.C.: Pan American Union, 1959.

Llewellyn, Richard. *How Green Was My Valley.* New York: Macmillan, 1967.

Zola, Emile. *Germinal.* Baltimore: Penguin Books, 1974.

Drama

Storey, David. *In Celebration.* New York: Grove, 1975.

Mining Lore and Ballads

Korson, George. *Minstrels of the Mine Patch: Songs and Stories of the Anthracite Industry.* Hatboro, Pennsylvania: Folklore Associates Inc., 1964.

Paul, Wolfgang. *Mining Lore.* Portland, Oregon: Morris Printing Co., 1970.

OF LOCAL INTEREST

Nonfiction
Bonosky, Frank J. "Anatomy of a Mine Disaster." *Mainstream*, June 1963, pp. 8–29.
Bracker, Milton. "Portrait in Black and White." *New York Times Magazine* 30 (November 1941): 5.
Gilfillan, Harriet W. *I Went to Pit College*. New York: Viking, 1934.
H. C. Frick Coke Company. *Connellsville Coke*. Pittsburgh, 1893.
Lauck, W. J. "Bituminous Coal Miner and Coke Worker of Western Pennsylvania." *Survey* 26 (1911): 34–51.
Maclean, Annie M. "Life in the Pennsylvania Coal Fields with Particular Reference to Women." *American Journal of Sociology* 14 (1909): 329–51.
Sheppard, Muriel. *Cloud by Day: The Story of Coal and Coke and People*. 1947. Reprint. Pittsburgh: University of Pittsburgh Press, 1991.

Fiction
Burgan, John, *The Long Discovery: A Novel*. New York: Farrar, Straus, 1950.
Campbell, Ed. *Between Heaven and Hell*. Chalk Hill, Pa.: The Campbell Family, 1990.
Lawrence, Oliver. "Beyond the Boundary Wall." In *Stanford Short Stories: Nineteen Forty-nine*, pp. 91–102. Stanford, Cal.: Stanford University Press, 1949.
Musmanno, Michael A. *Black Fury*. New York: Fountainhead Publishers, 1966.
Swift, Alfred M. "I'm Going Home." In *Post Stories of 1940*, pp. 44–55. Boston: Little, Brown, 1941.
Turnbull, Agnes Sligh. *Remember the End*. 1938. Reprint. New York: Avon, 1967.

Mining Lore and Ballads
Korson, George. *Coal Dust on the Fiddle: Songs and Stories of the Bituminous Industry*. Hatboro, Pennsylvania: Folklore Associates, Inc., 1965.

NARRATORS AND INTERVIEWERS

Narrators	Interviewers
Anonymous Miner	Daryl Walker
Badovinac, George	Albert Skomra
Billek, Andrew	Vinette Billek
Billek, Anna	Vinette Billek
Burke, William, Sr.	Dennis Brestensky
Calderone, Samuel	John Foor
Coll, John	Albert Skomra
Craft, Marie C.	Evelyn Hovanec
Dantzler, Howard	Evelyn Hovanec
Dolobach, Helen	Mary Hirko
Dolobach, Steve	Mary Hirko
Duran, Andrew J.	Dennis Brestensky
Duran, Rose	Margaret Skomra
Gamon, Ann	Patricia Romito
Guappone, Carmen	Dennis Brestensky
Guappone, Michael	Dennis Brestensky
Gugar, Michael	Mark Gaudiano
Herring, Asa	Melvin Nicklow
Holpit, John W.	Bobby Salitrik
Hovanec, Andrew	Evelyn Hovanec
Hudek, Charles	Dennis Brestensky and Evelyn Hovanec
Hunchuck, Mary A.	Jerome DeFrank
Hustosky, John	William Hustosky
Kazmierczak, Ann	Albert Skomra
Kazmierczak, Anthony	Albert Skomra
Kehoe, John	John Foor
Kline, Cindy R.	Jan Golden
Kline, John A.	Kenneth Gerhard
Ludrosky, Stephen A.	Vinette Billek
McFarland, John Ellis	Kenneth Gerhard
Machinsky, Stanley	Kimberly Collins
Malesky, Mary Margaret	Albert Skomra
Morgan, Bennie E.	Jan Golden
Moser, Raymond	Rita Swetz
Munk, Joseph	Mary Hirko
Murray, Albert	Debi Sabo
Murray, Mary	Debi Sabo
Nicklow, Ray M.	Melvin Nicklow

Narrators	Interviewers
Olsen, Merle	Linda Martin
Peters, Stephen	Dennis Brestensky
Petrisko, John	Susan Avera
Poplarcheck, Edward	Mary Hirko
Poplarcheck, Sue	Mary Hirko
Reilly, James A.	Margaret Reilly Skomra
Rerko, Joseph	Evelyn Hovanec
Rerko, Eleanor	Evelyn Hovanec
Ryan, Viola	Sharon Ryan
Santella, Leonard	Evelyn Hovanec
Schuessler, Jerry F.	Evelyn Hovanec
Schuessler, Nellie	Evelyn Hovanec
Seaton, Harold, Sr.	Linda Martin
Shuman, Andrew P., Sr.	Patricia Romito
Shuman, Mary	Patricia Romito
Skomra, Louis	Albert Skomra
Skomra, Tekla	Albert Skomra
Anonymous Miner	Jeffrey Spoljarick
Swetz, Johanna	Rita Swetz
Vrobel, Ann	Evelyn Hovanec
Vrobel, Paul	Evelyn Hovanec
Whoolery, Alex	Dennis Brestensky
Wilson, Rev. Andrew	Melvin Nicklow

FRENCH NAPOLEONIC LANCER REGIMENTS

Michael G. Head

ALMARK PUBLISHING CO. LTD., LONDON

First Published — December 1971

ISBN 0 85524 044 X (hard cover edition)
ISBN 0 85524 045 8 (paper covered edition)

By the same Author:
FRENCH NAPOLEONIC ARTILLERY

Printed in Great Britain by
Martins Press Ltd., Woodbridge Street, London EC1
for the publishers, Almark Publishing Co. Ltd.,
270 Burlington Road, New Malden, Surrey, KT3 4NL.

Introduction

THIS second volume of a series dealing in detail with the uniforms and dress of the French Imperial Army of the First Empire period is concerned solely with one of the most colourful arms, the lancer regiments, and takes in both the Guard and Line lancers of 1804 to 1815. These are described in separate parts. Brief coverage is given in Part 1 to organization and establishment of the regiments purely for general guidance, though actual tactics and regimental histories are beyond the scope of this book. A preliminary glance at the following pages will show that the uniforms and accoutrements were not only colourful but also of considerable complexity, both in style and in allocation. In many cases distinctions between ranks and companies, etc, were subtle, but in other cases the differences were of major importance. In addition to the rank and company distinctions there were many orders of dress from parade dress down to stable and fatigue orders. This book records most known styles, research including exhaustive study of contemporary records and archives.

Because the garments were themselves complicated in cut, most of the colour illustrations in this book show them laid out to reveal all the fundamental details of lace, piping, and braid; ordinary line drawings are used to show the appearance of the garments on the wearer and it is a fairly simple matter for the reader to make his own cross-references between colour plate and drawing to ascertain colour details where these are not already obvious. A further idea of the uniforms and appearance when in use is given by the photographs in both colour and black and white showing high-quality models from the Historex range of figures. Thanks are due to Mr Lynn Sangster of Historex Agents, Dover, for the kind loan of models and photographs for these illustrations.

Style in general follows that of the previous book in this series, *French Napoleonic Artillery*, and as before it is hoped that both military figure modellers and uniform enthusiasts will find this volume useful as a means of identifying the equipment and dress of the lancer regiments concerned.

CONTENTS

ABOVE: An officer of the 7th or 8th Regiment of Lancers of the Line in full dress, portrayed by a Historex model figure; a colour view is given on page 48. COVER: This model diorama from France shows a Polish Guard Lancer on the right and a trumpeter of the same regiment behind him (Lynn Sangster).

4

1: Regiments and Equipment

THE first lancer regiment to be formed and later issued with their national weapon were the *Chevau Legers Polonais de la Garde Imperiale*. When Napoleon entered Warsaw, he was escorted by a guard of honour composed of Polish noblemen and he was so impressed by their bearing that, in 1807, he ordered the formation of a regiment of Polish light horse. Comprising four squadrons and a headquarters, the regiment totalled 968 men. A squadron drawn up in two ranks covered 150 yards of frontage. The regiment was quartered at Chantilly and in 1809 the lance was issued. The unit was now named *1er Chevau Legers Lanciers Polonais*. At first all ranks carried the new weapon, but eventually only the first rank used the lance; that is 66 out of 125 men. The complete armament, therefore, of a Polish Lancer was the lance, sabre, pistols (carried under the shabraque), carbine and bayonet. When only the front rank was armed with the lance, they carried in addition a sabre and two pistols. The rear rank then carried the sabre, pistols, carbine and bayonet.

The brigadiers (corporals) of the front rank carried the original complete array of arms. Sous officers and trumpeters were armed with the sabre and pistols only.

In 1812 a fifth squadron was formed and the regiment now totalled 1,500 men. They saw service in Spain and most other campaigns, distinguishing themselves at Wagram in 1809. When Napoleon was exiled to Elba, 120 Polish Lancers accompanied him and later saw action at Ligny. The Colonel Major of the regiment was Baron Vincent Corvin Krasinski, formerly of Dombrowski's Polish Lancers.

The second Regiment of Lancers of the Guard were the *2eme Chevau Legers Lanciers* or 'Lanciers Rouges', so named after their scarlet uniform. Formed in 1810 from the Hussars of the Dutch Guard and the Dutch Garde du Corps, the regiment consisted of 748 men. In 1812 1,400 men of the 2nd Regiment saw service in Russia, and only a bare 200 returned from the debacle.

In January 1813 the regiment consisted of eight squadrons, each of 250 men. Later the squadron of the Dragoons of the Paris Municipal Guards were included, making a total of 2,500 men in 10 squadrons. The first four squadrons were composed mainly of Dutch, and ranked in the Middle Guard. The remaining squadrons were French and were part of the Young Guard. When formed in 1811 the men were armed with the lance, sabre and a pistol. In 1813 the Dutch Lancers followed the example of the Polish in arming only the front rank with the lance, sabre and pistol. The rear rank carried the sabre, pistol, carbine and bayonet. As with the Polish, only brigadiers in the front rank carried the full armament. Sous officers and trumpeters carried the sabre and pistols.

During the 100-day campaign culminating at Waterloo, the four squadrons

A superb diorama made with Historex models. From left to right can be seen Imperial Guard Dragoons, 2nd Regiment of Dutch Lancers (in gateway) with Imperial Guard Grenadiers à Cheval following them. The Grenadier presents arms and Napoleon and his staff review the column on the right (Lynn Sangster).

of Dutch Lancers, who had been taken into the Royal Guard, were placed with the Polish squadron under the name of *Chevau Legers Lanciers de la Garde Imperiale*.

A third regiment was formed in 1812, and dressed identically to the first but with yellow or gold lace. The regiment soon ceased to exist, being literally cut to pieces in Russia.

When Murat became Grand Duke of Berg, he ordered the formation of a regiment of *Chevau Legers*, part of which formed his personal body guard (Garde de Corps). Murat took his regiment to Spain and in November of 1808 the regiment was incorporated into the Imperial Guard. The regiment was then known as the *Chasseurs à Cheval de Berg*. In 1809 Napoleon decided to issue the lance to the *Chasseurs de Berg* and the *Lanciers de Berg* came into being. Service was mainly in Spain, but in 1812 the first three squadrons of the 2nd Regiment (the 2nd was formed in Germany) were part of the 30th Brigade, together with the Hessian and Saxon light horse. In 1813, after the successful advances of the Allies, the *Lanciers de Berg* became the *Hussars de Berg* under the victorious Allies, eventually ending up as the 11th Prussian Hussars.

Many Tartars had settled in Lithuania and in 1812 one Mustapha Achmatowicz was charged with forming a regiment of cavalry from these Muslims, to be named *Tartares Lithuaniens*. However, only a squadron could be raised and this was attached to the ill-fated 3rd Regiment of Polish Lancers under the command of General Konpka, where the men acted as scouts.

After the Russian campaign barely a company of the Tartares remained. At

Dresden there were 41 men and three officers. Eventually this small band was attached to the 3rd Regiment of Eclaireurs, and in 1814 when Napoleon abdicated they returned to their home in Lithuania.

Three regiments of Eclaireurs were raised in 1812 as scout lancers. Each regiment consisted of four squadrons of 250 men. The 1st and 2nd Regiments were recruited from existing Line regiments and the 3rd formed from Poles. The 1st Regiment was attached to the *Grenadiers à Cheval de la Garde* and recruited mainly from the *Guards d'Honneur*; the 2nd, recruited from 1,000 Imperial postillions, was attached to the *Dragoons de la Imperatrice*; and the 3rd was attached to the Polish Lancers. As will be seen in Part 3, although these regiments bore the same designation, their uniforms were all different. The 1st Regiment was divided into Old and Young Guard sections, but the 2nd and 3rd Regiments were ranked as Young Guard. In 1814 the first two regiments were returned to Line service and the 3rd returned to Poland.

The regiments of lancers of the Line were numbered consecutively 1 to 9. The first six regiments were French, while the 7th and 8th were Polish, formed from the Vistula Legion. The 9th was formed from the *30eme Chasseurs à Cheval* who were in the main German. The first six were formed in 1811 from the 1st, 3rd, 8th, 9th, 10th and 29th Regiments of Line Dragoons and were known as the *Lanciers Francais de la Ligne*. This reflects Napoleon's enthusiasm for the lance as a weapon—an enthusiasm not shared by many of the lancers.

The usual strength was four squadrons of 250 men each, divided into two companies of 125 men, of whom five were officers. When first raised, the *Chevau Legers Francais* were armed with the lance and the sabre, except for 30 men in each company of 120 who were armed with a carbine, bayonet and sabre. The latter were known as Carabiniers. Soon, however, all men carried lance, musket, sabre and bayonet. Sous officers only carried the musket and sabre, never the lance.

In 1807 the remnants of the Polish volunteers of the Italian Legion assembled in Westphalia, where the *Legion de la Vistula* was formed. Among the units formed were two regiments of lancers. The Legion fought in Spain and Russia, and in 1811 the Polish Lancers became the 7th and 8th Regiments of *Lanciers Polonais de la Ligne*. From 1808 to 1811 centre companies did not carry a musket, only a pistol, which was sometimes attached by the trigger guard to the swivel hook of the carbine belt. In 1811 the musket was issued to all companies and only the sous officers and trumpeters were excepted. They simply carried a sabre and pistols.

The 9th Regiment of Lancers originated from a unit formed in February of 1811 at Hamburg. This unit was the *30eme Chasseurs à Cheval*, who were unusual in that they were created as chasseurs-lanciers, wearing the czapska and kurtka with the lance as their main weapon. In June of the same year they were re-designated as the *9eme Regiment Lanciers Polonias de la Ligne*, although the majority of the men were German. They retained their colourful uniforms, however, until 1813 when the regulation dress was adopted in full. Disbanded in 1814 the Poles returned to their homeland.

The final units we are concerned with are the Gendarmerie units in Spain from 1810. From this year there were six legions of gendarmes in Spain to protect communications and supply routes, as well as actively hunting guerrilla units.

In the latter part of 1810, lancers were attached to the legions and their uniforms are described later in this book.

2: Basic Lancer Uniforms

THE standard lancers czapska originated in Poland and has always been a distinctive feature of most branches of the Polish armed forces. The square top was piped at the edges and from corner to corner across the top. Additionally, piping appeared on the sides running vertically down from each corner.

The cockade was worn just below the left front edge. The central part, where the narrowing top started to expand into the lower half known as the 'turban', was usually encircled by a band of lace. The lower part (turban) was invariably black. A black leather peak appeared at the front, which was sometimes edged or bound with metal. On each side of the turban, just to the rear of the peak, metal 'lions' heads' appeared which attached the curb chain chinstrap to the czapska. The chin chain could be unhooked from the right-hand side lion's head and hooked on to the top corner projecting to the right. This was usual only when dismounted.

Plumes (in any form) were fitted into a brass holder, which appears to have been inserted beneath the cockade or into the covering material itself. When cords were worn both ends had flattened woven flounders of oval shape with tasseled ends. The cord went around the base of the plume and draped down around the right-hand side of the czapska to the level of the centre band, encircled the czapska to rise again to the plume. This was repeated twice. The cords were, in fact, two cords together so the impression was of four cords surrounding the czapska. The cords were knotted around the base of the plume and could be worn extended to encircle the body, over one shoulder and under the arm on the opposite side, to prevent the loss of the czapska should it become dislodged from the wearer's head. This, in fact, was the original intention of all the plaited cords which decorated French Napoleonic headgear. At the front a sunray plate of brass and white metal was usually worn. Officers invariably had small metal lions' heads at the four corners of the top.

ABOVE, LEFT: Detail of czapska plate. CENTRE: Cockade, showing silver Polish cross. ABOVE, RIGHT: Czapska in weatherproof cover. See Plate 1 (page 33) for view without cover.

ABOVE, LEFT: Cylindrical shako (3rd Eclaireurs). ABOVE: Bell type shako with waterproof cover. ABOVE, RIGHT: Dragoon style forage cap. BELOW, LEFT: Details of dragoon style forage cap showing pointed flap. BELOW, RIGHT: Details of Pokalem forage cap.

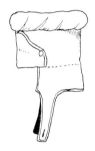
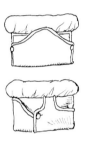

The shako was made of felt and leather and was about 217mm high with a top diameter of about 270mm. The top, and band around the top, were of leather as was the lower band which had a small buckle at the back to allow the fit to be adjusted. Metal plates of varying designs were worn at the front below the cockade. Plumes and pompoms were affixed above the cockade. A varnished leather peak, sometimes edged with metal, was fixed at the front. At either side of the shako metal chin scales were attached by bosses or rosaces. The chin scales tied below the chin, or on many occasions were tied up behind the plume.

The cylindrical shako (Plate 3) of 1812 as worn by units of the Eclaireurs, was taller than the bell-shaped shako and, as the name implies, was perfectly cylindrical from top to bottom. Construction was similar to the bell shako but simpler, and it was cheaper to manufacture. At the back a leather stiffening plate was worn and the cockade appeared midway between top and bottom with a lace strip from the top of the shako fastening to a button in the centre of the cockade. Black leather chin straps with adjusting buckles were normally worn but metal chin scales fastening to rosaces at either side, again midway between top and bottom, were also used, probably mainly by officers.

From a button at the rear top, cords draped down over the back and encircled the body, over one shoulder and under the arm at the other side. This was to secure the shako should it be dislodged. Oilskin covers were worn over all the above-mentioned headgear on campaign or in foul weather.

The cockade was of red, white and blue in the following order: centre blue,

9

then red, then white outer. The exception in this volume are the *Lanciers de Berg* who wore their national cockade of a red centre and narrow white outer.

Forage caps were of two types, the dragoon style which was the most common, and the Pokalem which appeared later. The dragoon-style cap was basically a fore and aft cap with a long pointed flap. The Pokalem cap was circular with a flap that could be lowered to cover the neck and ears, buttoning under the chin.

Variations on headgear, peculiar to specific regiments (eg, French Line Lancer Helmets) are dealt with in the appropriate chapters.

We are basically concerned with three main types of coatee. These are the Kurtka, the Habit Veste and the chasseur coatee or Habit Kinski. Again variations and specific exceptions are dealt with fully as they appear.

The Kurtka was the classic lancer coat, of Polish origin and is shown in Plates 1, 2 and 5. The Kurtka had single turnbacks similar to those of the standard British uniform of the time, but larger. The seams at the back and down the arms were piped as were the three pointed pocket flaps. Cuffs were

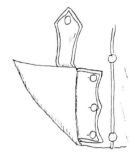

LEFT: Kurtka with lapels crossed. RIGHT: Detail of girdle strap on kurtka (see text). BELOW: Half-round button worn on kurtka.

pointed with two buttons above, at the rear. Buttons also appeared at the rear waist, on the piping and at the rear bottom. The lapels at the front could be worn in two ways. First, the full-dress style, which showed the full facing colour, the lapels were folded back and hooked down the centre. Secondly, on campaign, etc, the lapels could cross over and button. In this case only a narrow edge of colour showed on the buttoned side. On the lapels there were six large buttons on either side and another on each side near the collar. On the shoulders a small button and a strap appeared to locate the shoulder strap, in whatever form it took. The stand-up collar was quite tall and hooked at the front. On the left side a girdle strap, similar to a shoulder strap, was worn just forward of the pocket and above the turnback. This supported the sword belt, which would tend otherwise to droop with the weight of the sword.

The Habit Veste was very similar in appearance to the kurtka having a straight-cut front as opposed to the habit coat which was cut away. The collar was lower and the pointed cuffs usually carried three buttons, one on the cuff and two above. The arrangement of the lapels was identical to the kurtka and could be worn in either of the two styles previously mentioned. There was no piping, however, to the seams at the rear and the coat had double turnbacks. Two styles of pockets were used and no definitive rule can be made as to which was used by any particular regiment. It seems probable that most would be a mixture of the two styles. First there was the three-pointed flap pocket and secondly the Soubisse pocket. Both styles are shown in Plate 4, and

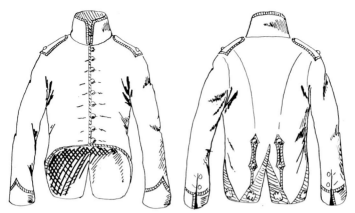

ABOVE: Typical Habit Kinski, this one being worn by the 1st and 2nd Eclaireurs. FOOT OF PAGE: Cloak (note slit at rear to allow it to fall either side of horse) and regulation great coat.

it will be noticed that the waist button is edged by the Soubisse pocket piping.

The chasseur coatee or Habit Kinski was in many respects similar to the Habit Veste, but was a single-breasted garment buttoning at the front with a row of eight buttons and piped down the front edge and bottom. The bottom edge was not straight cut but curved down towards the turnbacks. It is almost certain that only Soubisse pockets were used, but the element of doubt does exist that the three-pointed flap pocket may have appeared. On the pointed cuffs only two buttons appeared, one on and one above the cuff.

Great coats and cloaks were usually cut very fully to allow room for the equipment worn underneath and in both cases the shoulders were covered by a detachable cape. Buttons on the kurtka were domed while those on the other coats were normally flat.

Lancer trousers were cut very tight fitting and had two stripes at each

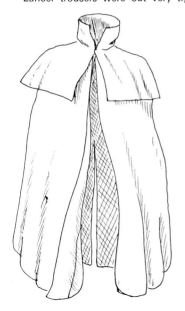

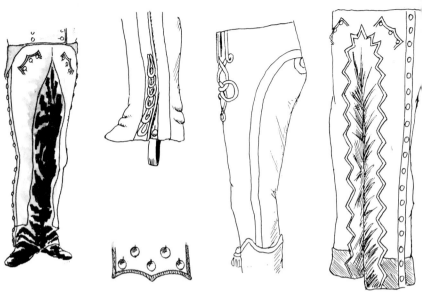

ABOVE, LEFT TO RIGHT: Pantalons à cheval, detail of five button pocket on pantalons (lower), lancers' open-ended trousers (overalls), hussar-style breeches, pantalons à cheval with zig-zag leather inserts.

outside seam with piping separating them. The bottoms were open at the seams to allow the feet to pass through. The open slits were then fastened by cord loops and buttons.

Hussar-style breeches were also tight fitting and had stripes on the outside seam which curved around on to the rear of the trousers, where they met and formed a ring. At the front they were usually decorated by Hungarian knots or spearheads. Officers had spearheads, the number of laces being indicative of rank, as shown.

Campaign dress consisted of either *pantalons à cheval* (which normally buttoned down the outside seams) or overalls which were pulled on. In most cases (except for certain of the officers) the inside leg and seat were reinforced with leather, which also extended completely around the bottoms. Various types are shown in the drawings.

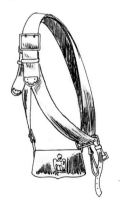

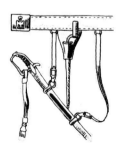

LEFT: Carbine and pouch belts. ABOVE: Waist belt showing attachment of sword bayonet.

12

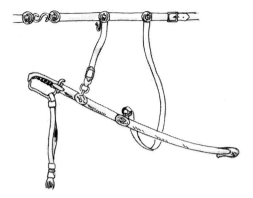

LEFT: Hungarian belt, officer's type.

Shoulder pouch belts were usually of whitened leather (50mm wide), which showed fawny natural leather colour on the underside, and fastened by a buckle of brass behind the shoulder. The end passed through a brass slide and was reinforced at the tip by a brass plate, as shown in the drawing.

The carbine belt which was wider than the pouch belt (98mm wide), was of the same material and fastened in the same manner. Details of the belt and of the carbine swivel hook are given in the drawings.

Two types of sword belt were common to the regiments we are describing. First, the waist belt (67mm wide) which was fastened with an oblong metal plate and, secondly, the Hungarian belt (35mm wide) which was worn over the hips, as shown here (above).

The light cavalry sabre was used (102cm long) by all the regiments (except the *Tartares Lithuaniens*, who carried a Mameluke sword) with two styles of hilts. The earlier version was the single bar type, while the later version had three bars which covered the hand more fully and, therefore, afforded greater protection (see Plate 9, page 54).

The light cavalry carbine was about 115cm long from muzzle to stock. The stock plate and the metal fitting at the front were of brass. The centre binding was iron, as was the carrying ring and slide. The firing mechanism was mainly iron but with some brass fittings. The trigger guard was brass. The methods of attaching the carbine to the belt and also the method of carrying fixed to the saddle are shown in the drawings.

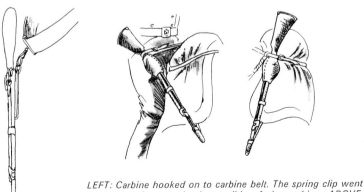

LEFT: Carbine hooked on to carbine belt. The spring clip went through a ring on the brass slide of the carbine. ABOVE: Alternative methods of carrying the carbine.

13

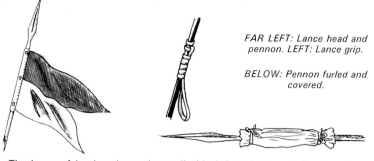

FAR LEFT: Lance head and
pennon. LEFT: Lance grip.

BELOW: Pennon furled and
covered.

The lance of hardened wood, usually black in colour, was 2m 2cm long from point to butt. At the point of balance a wrist strap of white leather was attached. This strap was also wound around the lance to provide a hand grip. The pennon was affixed to three iron studs and measured 73cm along the top, 38cm deep and 37cm to the centre of the swallow tail. Descriptions of the *Tartares Lithuaniens* dress and of Eclaireur regiments are given fully in the following pages.

IMPERIAL LIVERY

The Emperor decided in 1812 to allow all Line trumpeters to wear his Imperial livery. Units based in France and near their headquarters were quick to wear this new uniform, but regiments or squadrons on service presented a mixed appearance. Replacements would be wearing the new style while the older men would still have their colourful uniforms. It is, therefore, impossible to say when, if it ever did, become the standard dress for trumpeters. The various differences applicable to each regiment are given in the text and we will, therefore, only describe the lace itself and mention that the basic coat colour was dark green.

There are two known styles of Imperial lace, the first to be described, however, being the most common. Basically a yellow lace with scarlet edges, the lace was divided horizontally by black into rectangules. In alternate areas appeared a green eagle and a green 'N'. Whether the actual lace was worn vertically or horizontally, the 'Ns' and the eagles were always vertical, so there were two patterns. When worn in two strips together (eg, across the breast) the laces were usually separated by a white cord.

The second, and least known style, was similar to the first but had narrower scarlet edges and the 'N' was in yellow on a green ground. The eagle remained green on yellow.

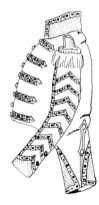

FAR LEFT: Detail of the two styles of Imperial Livery lace described above. LEFT: Trumpeter's coatee, Lancers de Berg, showing Imperial Livery with lace on dark green. Collar, cuffs, turnbacks, and soubisse pocket piping in Rose Red.

14

3: Lancer Regiments of the Guard

WHEN originally formed from the Consular Guard, the Imperiai Guard was in fact a small *élite* organization. It eventually grew in size by the addition of further regiments until it became an army in its own right. The Guard was in turn divided into the Old Guard, Middle Guard and Young Guard. The Old Guard, in particular, enjoyed much higher rates of pay and in general the uniforms and equipment were of a higher quality than that supplied to the Line. Towards the end of the Empire, standards declined with the immense losses suffered by Napoleon, and many of the later regiments added were little better equipped than the ordinary Line Regiments. The Lancers of the Guard, however, maintained a very high standard until the end. The first regiment of Lancers in the Guard was the 1st Regiment of *Chevau Legers Lanciers Polonais de la Garde*, details of whose uniforms are shown in Plate 1.

HEADGEAR
The Polish czapska was worn with the upper part in crimson cloth with white piping around the edge, at the corners and crossing corner to corner on the top. A strip of white lace encircled the centre portion. The lower part, called the turban, was black and at the front there was a black leather peak edged with white metal. Above the peak appeared a large brass plate which took the form of sunrays. At the lower centre part of the plate appeared a white metal area upon which there was a brass 'N' with a brass crown above it. A tall white plume was worn in a white metal holder above the tricolour cockade. The cockade had a blue centre, then red, then white at the edge. Superimposed on the cockade was a silver Polish cross. The cords and flounders were white and the chin chain was of white metal, lined with crimson cloth.

The czapskas worn by *Marechals des Logis* and *Marechals des Logis Chefs* had mixed silver and crimson cords and flounders.

Trumpeters wore a czapska with a crimson upper half, piped white and with silver lace around the centre. The turban was black and the chin strap and lion heads were brass. The peak was also edged in brass. The cords and flounders were mixed white and silver and a white plume was carried. In 1810 this style of czapska was replaced by one with a white upper part, piped

LEFT: Method of fastening officers' cloaks—see page 17.

15

1st Regiment Polish Lancers of the Guard
(1me Regiment Chevau Legers Lancier Polonnais de la Garde)

LEFT TO RIGHT: Lancer, full dress. Lancer in campaign dress with pantalons à cheval and rolled great coat. Lancer in great coat and field service cap. Officer in full dress; trousers were crimson.

crimson. The lace band remained silver and the cords and flounders were mixed crimson and silver. The curb chain, lion heads and the edging to the peak was silver in place of the brass used before. The plume also changed, being crimson with a white tip. Officers wore an identical czapska to the men, but had silver piping in place of the white. The chin chain and edging to the peak was also silver. Contemporary prints show some officers with a fawn-covered czapska when on the march, but the normal black oilskin was also used.

KURTKAS

The close-fitting short jacket worn by the lancers was of Polish origin. In the case of the 1st Regiment the kurtka was coloured dark blue with the collar, lapels, pointed cuffs, turnbacks and the piping on the rear seams of crimson (Plate 1). The lapels were edged with white lace. The domed buttons were of white material. The girdle strap at the left waist was also blue, piped crimson. Until 1809, when the lance was introduced, a white epaulette was worn on the right shoulder and a white full epaulette on the left. In 1809 these positions were reversed. For full dress wear the lapels were buttoned back at each side and hooked together down the centre of the chest. For *tenue de marche* and service wear the lapels crossed over each other, thus only showing an edging of crimson at the side which was buttoned. This could be either the right or left side depending on the period as the kurtka was buttoned down at the side which carried the aiguillette, the ends of which were attached to the top buttonhole. Details of the variations to rank are shown in Appendix 4.

Trumpeters wore a crimson kurtka with a white collar, lapels, cuffs, turnbacks and piping. Silver lace edged the collar, lapels and cuffs. The aiguillette worn on the right shoulder, and the epaulette worn on the left were mixed white and silver, the strap of the epaulette being silver. In *tenue de route* the lapels were crossed over, as already described, buttoning on the right with a white edging showing on that side.

As with the czapskas the colours of the kurtka underwent a change in 1810, and from that time the kurtka was white with crimson facings. The collar, lapels and cuffs again carried silver lace edging. Additionally the buttonholes on the lapels had silver lace 'brandenbergs' (see drawing). The aiguillette worn on the right side was silver with a crimson stripe on the strap, a crimson half moon and mixed silver and crimson fringes.

Detail of aiguillette of Marechal des Logis,
1st Polish Lancers of the Guard.

The kurtka described above was for full dress wear only, and on service a sky blue uniform was worn with crimson collars, lapels, turnbacks, cuffs and piping. There was silver lace on the collar, lapels and cuffs. In this case, however, there were no brandenbergs. In *tenue de marche* the service dress uniform was worn with the lapels crossed over and buttoned on the left, with an edge of crimson showing. The epaulettes and aiguillettes worn with the service dress were identical to those worn on the full dress uniform.

Officers wore an identical uniform to that of the men but of a better quality material with the addition of silver lace, of the pattern shown in the drawing, to the collar, lapels, cuffs and turnbacks. Buttons were silver. In *tenue de route* the lapels were crossed over, buttoning at the right side.

On parade the Colonel and Major wore a white kurtka with crimson collar, lapels, cuffs, turnbacks and piping. Silver lace was applied to the edges of the collar, lapels, cuffs and turnbacks.

Rank markings are shown in the drawings and tables in Appendix 4.

CLOAKS

The men wore a white greatcoat, coming to below the knee and with a slit at the back to facilitate riding. The collar of the greatcoat was crimson and around the shoulders was attached a short white cape. The coat fastened with five cloth-covered buttons and the cape had three cloth-covered buttons. The field service cap was crimson with white lacing and the pointed flap was blue piped and tasseled white. Officers wore a blue cloak with a crimson collar. The cloak was fastened by a silver chain at the neck.

TROUSERS

The men wore, in full dress, tight-fitting trousers of blue with two crimson stripes down the outside of each leg. These stripes were separated by a crimson welt, so no blue showed between. The bottoms of the trousers was slit open on the outside seam to allow the feet to pass through. This opening was closed by means of loops and cloth-covered buttons in crimson. On the march or on service, *pantalons à cheval* were usually worn over the trousers. These were cut much more fully than the trousers, with the inside leg and the

bottoms of the legs reinforced by black leather inserts. The pantalons fastened down the outside of each leg by 18 white metal buttons, beneath which was a single crimson stripe. Two pockets were set at angles at the front and they had three pointed flaps which fastened with three white metal buttons. The flaps were piped crimson.

Trumpeters wore crimson trousers with white stripes and piping with both of the kurtkas already described. With the sky blue service dress, however, they wore sky blue trousers with crimson stripes. Pantalons were identical to those of the men during the period 1807–10. With the introduction of the sky blue service dress, however, they became sky blue with a crimson stripe. Officers wore identical trousers to the men but with the stripes and piping in silver. For parade wear officers had crimson trousers with silver stripes. When worn the pantalons were the same as the men's. In all cases black leather boots were worn. The men and trumpeters had blackened iron spurs, the officers silver.

EQUIPMENT AND ACCESSORIES

A whitened leather waist belt was worn by the men which was fastened by a brass oblong plate at the front. A black leather pouch was carried on a white shoulder belt. The flap of the pouch carried a brass crowned eagle upon it (Plate 10). Where applicable a carbine belt was worn over the pouch belt.

OPPOSITE PAGE: Historex model of a lancer of 1me Chevau Legers Lanciers de la Garde. ABOVE: Brigadier of the regiment in full dress. Though the chevrons of rank are concealed by the gloves, the rank is also indicated by the lace on the collar. INSET, TOP: Detail of officer's lace. INSET, BOTTOM: Stirrup detail showing lance bucket. INSET, CENTRE: Method of fastening officer's sash—see description in text, page 20. INSET, ABOVE: Detail of halter, rein, and bridle.

A light cavalry pattern sabre, usually with a single bar guard, was carried. The sabre had a brass hilt with a white sword knot. The scabbard was also brass with a black leather insert between the sling rings. Where a carbine was issued, a bayonet was carried in a brown leather scabbard which was fastened to the waist belt between the sabre straps. Until 1809 the carbine was carried on the right-hand side of the saddle, when with the introduction of the lance it moved to the left side. The carbine was supported in a black leather bucket, into which the muzzle fitted. Around the small of the butt a brown leather strap passed which fastened on to the saddle, passing through the saddle cloth. The firing mechanism was protected from the elements by a white canvas cover.

The lance pennon was crimson over white. On the march the pennon was furled around the lance and secured by a black cover which tied in two places.

Trumpeters wore basically the same equipment as the men but were never issued with a carbine, so they did not have a carbine belt. The trumpeters' sword knot was mixed silver and white until 1810 when, in line with the rest of the uniform, it became silver and crimson. Gauntlet gloves were worn by men and trumpeters, with ochre gloves and white gauntlets.

From 1807–10 the trumpet itself was silver-plated with mixed white and silver cords and tassels. In 1810 the cords became crimson and silver, and a crimson trumpet banner was attached to the trumpet for parade use. This banner had on one face a gold eagle superimposed over a silver 'sunburst' and encircled by silver laurel leaves. On the reverse was a gold crowned 'N' inside a silver wreath, the whole encircled by silver laurel leaves. The banner was fringed on each edge by mixed silver and crimson fringes as shown in Plate 1.

Officers wore a silver sash terminating in two large tassels which hung down at the right side where the sash tied. With this sash a Hungarian sword belt was worn covered in silver lace. For normal wear, ie, not parade, the sash was not used and in place of the Hungarian belt a silver-laced waist belt was used which fastened by means of a silver plate which had embossed on it a gilt eagle. The sabre had a silver hilt and sword knot and was carried in a silver scabbard.

The pouch belt was covered in silver lace and on the chest were gilt ornaments as shown in Plate 10. The pouch itself was also silver covered with gilt edging to the flap and a gilt 'sunburst' on the flap. In *tenue de marche* the pouch belt usually had a red leather cover around it fastened with silver buttons down the centre. Officers wore all-white gauntlets or wrist gloves.

HORSE FURNITURE

The men had a blue cloth shabraque. At the extreme edge was a line of crimson piping, then a line of white piping and a broad crimson stripe, on the inner edge of which was another line of white piping (Plate 6). In the rear pointed corners of the shabraque, set at an angle of 45°, was a white crowned

LEFT: Details of shabraque ornamentation as described in text.

eagle. At the front of the shabraque, where it bulged with the cloak under it, were set white crowned 'Ns' (drawing, page 20). A cylindrical valise of crimson was carried which was piped and laced white at the round ends. The rubbing plates at the side of the shabraque, where the rider's knees rested, were black. The girth, ie, the strap which retained the saddle, was grey. The surcingle which went over the shabraque and around the horse, almost covering the girth, was black. The remainder of the horse straps, including the reins and bridles, were black except for the stirrup leathers which were off-white. All buckles and studs were of iron and the stirrups themselves were blackened. On the outside of each stirrup a black leather lance butt was fitted to support the weight of the lance.

Trumpeters had a crimson shabraque with a white stripe and piping. The shabraque and valise were decorated in the same manner as the men's. The trumpeters always rode grey horses (Plate 6).

Officers had a blue shabraque edged with crimson piping and a silver lace stripe. Senior officers had inside the silver stripe another half stripe the width of the outer one. The eagles and 'Ns' were silver (Plate 6). The saddle itself was covered with panther skin and there were red stirrup leathers and silver stirrups. The snaffle rein was covered with silver lace, while the remaining horse straps were of black leather with silver buckles and silver ornaments. A valise was not carried on parade but for service use was crimson piped and laced with silver.

The Red Lancers
(Lancier Rouges)

The second of the Guard Lancer Regiments to be formed was the Red Lancers in 1810.

Before going into details of the uniform worn for the major part of their existence it is necessary to give a brief description of the uniform when the Royal Dutch Hussars became the *2eme Regiment Chevau Legers Lanciers*.

Shako was black, with no shako plate at the front but with yellow cords and flounders. A black plume, without a pompom, surmounted the usual tricolour cockade, which had a yellow retaining strap. The peak was of black leather and was edged with brass and the chin scales were also of brass. A scarlet Habit Coat was worn with long tails. The collar was blue as were the pointed cuffs. The lapels and turnbacks were scarlet piped blue, and the soubisse pockets were also piped blue. On the left shoulder a yellow aiguillette was worn, while on the right a yellow trefoil shoulder strap appeared. A scarlet waistcoat with yellow braiding and three rows of buttons was worn under the coat. Hussar-style breeches were worn with a yellow stripe at the sides and yellow Hungarian knots at the front. The Hungarian boots were in black leather trimmed and tasselled with yelow. A light cavalry sabre was carried with a brass hilt and a brass scabbard. The sword knot was yellow. The Hungarian sword belt and the pouch and carbine belts were of ochre-coloured leather, while the pouch was plain black. Horse furniture consisted of a blue cloth shabraque and valise with a yellow stripe. The greatcoat at this time was sky blue with a scarlet collar and was the same style as that used by the Polish Lancers. Gauntlet gloves were ochre coloured.

When the regiment changed its title the same basic colours were retained, but adapted to the Polish style.

HEADGEAR

The czapska worn by the men of the Old Guard had a scarlet upper part, a yellow lace centre band and a black turban. The piping on the top half was yellow. The peak was of black leather with brass edging. The chin chain was also of brass lined with scarlet cloth. A brass sunray plate appeared above the peak. The cords and flounders were yellow and the plume was white. No cross appeared on the tricolour cockade (Plate 2). As with the Polish Lancers a black oilskin cover was worn over the czapska when on the march. *Marechals des Logis* and *Marechals des Logis Chefs* had identical czapskas but with cords and flounders of mixed gold and scarlet. Young Guard squadrons wore an identical czapska but in place of the sunray plate carried a large brass 'N'. The czapskas of Velites (trainees) were the same as the Old Guard squadrons but with mixed blue and yellow cords and flounders. Their plume also differed, being black with a white tip.

Trumpeters wore a czapska with a white upper half, piped scarlet, a gold lace centre band and a black turban. The usual sunray plate appeared over the peak which was of black leather edged with brass. The cords and flounders were mixed gold and scarlet while the plume was white with a scarlet tip. The oilskin cover was donned on the march. Officers wore a czapska identical to the men's, but in place of the yellow piping and yellow cords gold was used. These uniform details are shown in Plate 2.

2eme Regiment Chevau Leger Lanciers

LEFT TO RIGHT: Czapska, Young Guard Squadron. Uniform worn when first formed from the Royal Dutch Hussar Regiment. Lancer of Young Guard Squadron. Brigadier in Grande Tenue INSET, LEFT: Detail of cockade and strap, Royal Dutch Hussar Regiment.

22

Lancer of 2nd Dutch (or Red) Lancers in campaign dress. Note czapska cover, blouse, water bottle, and furled and covered lance pennon (Historex model by Shepherd Paine).

COATS

The kurtka worn by the men of the Old Guard and Velites was scarlet with the collar, lapels, cuffs, turnbacks and piping dark blue. The buttons were of brass. There was an aiguillette on the left shoulder and a full epaulette on the right, both were yellow. The half moon above the fringes was blue. The Velites had epaulettes with blue shoulder straps edged with yellow lace. The half moons were blue and the fringes yellow. The aiguillette was mixed blue and yellow. On service the lapels were crossed over, showing an edge of blue. Another garment worn in *tenue de route* was a sky blue blouse, double breasted with two rows of nine brass buttons spaced equidistantly. The collar was scarlet and the plain round cuffs were sky blue.

The Young Guard squadrons wore a kurtka with the colours reversed. That is the kurtka was blue with scarlet collar, lapels, cuffs, turnbacks and piping. No aiguillettes or epaulettes were worn. Instead, pointed blue shoulder straps, piped scarlet, appeared on both shoulders. One source, however, does suggest yellow contra epaulettes, but this appears unlikely.

The trumpeters wore for full dress a white kurtka with a scarlet collar, lapels, cuffs, turnbacks and piping. The collar, lapels and cuffs were edged with gold lace and the lapels, buttonholes were trimmed with gold lace brandenbergs. An aiguillette of mixed gold and scarlet was attached to the left shoulder while on the right a full epaulette was worn. This had a scarlet strap edged with gold lace, the half-moons were gold and the fringes were mixed gold and scarlet. For service wear, the trumpeters wore a sky blue kurtka with scarlet collar, lapels, cuffs, turnbacks and piping. A gold lace edging appeared on the collar

23

FAR LEFT: Ecru coloured overalls worn by 2nd Dutch Lancers in summer. LEFT: Sky blue blouse worn on the march, as shown in picture on previous page.

and lapels. The epaulettes and aiguillettes were identical to those worn with the full dress uniform. In *tenue de route*, service dress was worn, sometimes with the lapels crossed over.

Officers wore the same uniform as the men with the addition of gold lace edging to the collar, lapels, cuffs and turnbacks for senior officers (Colonel and Major). The only other differences were the gold epaulettes of rank (see Appendix 4) and gilt buttons in place of brass. In *tenue de route* it was again usual for the lapels to be crossed over.

TROUSERS

The tight-fitting trousers were of the same cut as those described for the Polish Lancers and were issued to all squadrons. They were scarlet with two broad blue stripes separated by a scarlet welt. In *tenue de route*, *pantalons* à *cheval* could be worn with the kurtka and they were blue with black leather inserts. They fastened down the outside seam with 18 brass buttons, riding upon a single scarlet stripe. At the front two pockets were set at angles, each with three pointed flaps piped scarlet. After 1813 there appears to have been five brass buttons on each flap in place of the more usual three. In *tenue de été* (summer dress with the sky blue blouse) creamy fawn overalls were worn. They did not have leather inserts and buttoned down the outside seams with 18 cloth buttons. Young Guard squadrons wore the same trousers and pantalons as the Old Guard already described.

The trumpeters wore scarlet trousers with the full dress kurtka, but in place of the blue stripes their stripes were of gold lace and the central welt was also gold. For service dress the trousers were sky blue with two scarlet stripes separated by a sky blue welt. In *tenue de route*, pantalons were worn.

Officers had scarlet trousers with gold lace stripes and a scarlet central welt. In *tenue de route* officers appear to have usually worn blue trousers with a single gold lace stripe on the outer seams.

EQUIPMENT

The belts carried by the Red Lancers was identical to those carried by the Polish Lancers except that the Young Guard squadrons had a plain black pouch without the eagle badge. The lance pennon was, in the case of the Dutch, white above scarlet. The carbine was always carried at the left side. The

LEFT: Colonel, 2nd Dutch Lancers. The gold and scarlet sash and panther skin saddle are clearly shown (Historex model). BELOW, LEFT TO RIGHT: A lancer in summer campaign dress (tenue d'eté). A velite—the aiguillette, epaulette, and czapska cords were mixed blue and yellow. Lancer in summer campaign dress wearing kurtka and rolled great coat. INSET, BELOW: Velite's czapska.

field service cap was blue with yellow lacing and the top flap was scarlet piped and tasselled yellow.

A greatcoat, similar to that described for the Polish Lancers, was worn but in sky blue with a scarlet collar. Young Guard squadrons also wore an identical garment but coloured creamy fawn with a scarlet collar.

The full dress pouch belt for the trumpeters was covered with gold lace and had three narrow scarlet stripes. The pouch itself was the same as the men's (Plate 10). The waist belt was also gold with three scarlet stripes, while the sword knot was white with a tassel of mixed gold and scarlet. The service dress equipment consisted of the full dress pouch belt and a Hungarian sword belt of red leather, edged gold. In 1813 identical pouch and waist belts to the troops were worn in *tenue de route*. The trumpet was brass with mixed scarlet and gold cords and tassels. The trumpet banner carried on parade was of blue cloth, fringed with gold and shaped similar to a lance pennon. On the face appeared a gold crowned eagle beneath a silver scroll which was lined with scarlet. Clusters of leaves appeared in the points of the banner. On the reverse the banner was identical, except that a gold crowned 'N' replaced the eagle.

An interesting figure of a *Trompette-Major* is shown by Bacquoy (page 28). The first item of interest is that the figure is shown wearing a white fur colpack

BELOW: Another view of a lancer of the 2nd Dutch Lancers in campaign dress, this time wearing a kurtka with lapels crossed and pantalons à cheval. Compare with drawings on page 25. RIGHT: Trumpeter of 2nd Dutch Lancers in service dress, circa 1814. Note the grey horse. (Historex model).

26

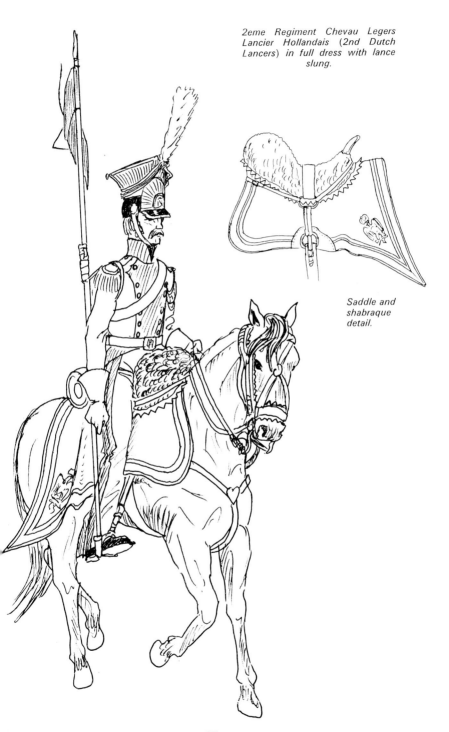

2eme Regiment Chevau Legers Lancier Hollandais (2nd Dutch Lancers) in full dress with lance slung.

Saddle and shabraque detail.

Trompette-Major, 2nd Dutch Lancers in 1811. See text for description.

with a scarlet bag. The bag, cords and flounders (worn on the left) were mixed gold and scarlet. A scarlet plume with a white tip was worn on the left. The kurtka has three gold laces edging the collar and the cuffs, but no brandenbergs on the lapels. The trumpet also differs from the norm in having four gold tassels in place of two. The scarlet shabraque is piped gold with two gold stripes (in the style of the men) instead of the single stripe normally used. All other details are the same as the full dress trumpeters already described. This figure is, incidentally, dated 1811.

Officers wore a gold laced pouch belt with a gilded pouch, the flap of which was in red leather with a gilt eagle and gold lace around the edge. Silver ornaments were worn on the front of the pouch belt (Plate 10). For full dress a gold sash interwoven with blue was carried around the waist and tied at the left side. With the sash a gold laced Hungarian sword belt was worn. On service the waist belt was white with gold lace edges and a gilt eagle was embossed on a silver plate. The sword straps were also white, edged with gold (Plate 10). The sabre itself had a gilt hilt and was carried in an iron scabbard with gilt rings and supports. The sword knot was in gold lace. In *tenue de route* a plain white waist belt identical to the men's was worn and the pouch belt was covered by red leather which buttoned with brass buttons down the centre (Plate 10). Officers wore a blue cloak or greatcoat.

HORSE FURNITURE

A cloth shabraque with pointed rear ends was used and was dark blue. The extreme edge was piped yellow, inside which were two yellow stripes, the inner one being half the width of the outer. Set at an angle of 45° in the rear corners were yellow crowned eagles. The saddle area was covered by a black sheepskin which had a yellow vandyking to its edges. A circular valise was carried, coloured scarlet with yellow piping and lacing (Plate 6).

The Young Guard squadrons had the same style shabraque, but with only a single yellow stripe and no piping. There was also no yellow vandyking to the sheepskin.

For full dress wear and for service wear, the trumpeters had a scarlet shabraque with yellow piping at the edges, inside which was a single gold lace stripe. Gold eagles were carried in the rear corners. The sheepskin was white, again with yellow vandyking. No valise was carried on parade, but for normal use a scarlet valise with gold piping and lace was carried (Plate 6). In 1813–14 the same shabraque as the men was used in *tenue de route*.

The officers had a similar shabraque to the men but with gold piping and lacing. The sheepskin was replaced by a panther-skin saddle cover. On the officers' shabraque the rubbing plates and straps were red as was the surcingle. Red leather stirrup straps were used and the officers stirrups were gilt. The bridle and harness was black with gilt studding and ornaments. A scarlet vandyked cloth lining showed beneath the halter. The snaffle bridle and reins were covered in gold lace.

The men and trumpeters had black leather rubbing plates and a black leather surcingle. The girth in all cases was grey. The stirrup straps were white and the stirrups of blackened iron. The men had black leather lance buckets on each stirrup. The remaining reins and bridles, etc, were black with brass buckles and ornaments. The halter was again lined with vandyked scarlet cloth.

All trumpeters rode grey horses. A third regiment of Polish Lancers was formed in July 1812, but were virtually wiped out in the Russian campaign. The survivors were merged with the 1st in 1813. Their uniforms were identical to the 1st Regiment but with yellow and gold in place of white and silver.

Lancers de Berg

The next regiment of lancers to be incorporated into the Guard was a colourful unit that became the *Lancers de Berg*. It is necessary to describe the uniforms used both prior to incorporation, when the unit was the *Chevau Legers de Berg*, and after as the *Lancers de Berg*. As there exists a certain amount of confusion as to the uniforms worn it is necessary to deal with individual uniforms in their entirety rather than in the style which has been used previously.

Chevau Legers de Berg: A uniform of the same style as the Polish Lancers was worn. The czapska had an amarante (light crimson of a rose tint) upper part, piped white. The centre band was white and the turban black. The familiar sunray plate appeared at the front and the peak was edged with brass. The cockade was white with a red centre and the plume was white. Chin chains were brass and cords and flounders were white. The kurtka was white with amarante collar, lapels, cuffs, turnbacks and piping. Trousers were amarante with two white stripes separated by a welt of amarante. Buttons were of white metal. A white epaulette was worn on the left shoulder and a white aiguillette on the right. A plain black pouch was attached to a whitened shoulder belt. A single bar light cavalry sabre with the hilt and scabbard was suspended from

Chevaux Legers de Berg (Lancers de Berg)
LEFT TO RIGHT: Lancer in campaign dress, 1807-08. Garde du Corps Company man in full dress, 1807-08. Kettle-drummer, 1807-08. Lancer of the Elite Company circa 1813.

30

LEFT: Kettle-drum banner in amarante cloth with silver lace decorations. RIGHT: Kettle-drummer's stirrups.

a white waist belt, which fastened by a brass belt plate embossed with an eagle. The sword knot was white.

One squadron formed Murat's *Garde du Corps* and had, in addition, white lace edging to the collar, lapels and cuffs. The lapel buttonholes also had white lace brandenbergs added.

Trumpeters wore the same uniform as the men, but with the kurtka coloured amarante with white collar, lapels, cuffs, turnbacks and piping. Around the collar, lapels and cuffs was silver lacing. The trumpet was brass with mixed white and silver cords and tassels. A white trumpet banner was carried on parade with a silver crowned eagle on both faces and edged with silver fringes. The plume was white with a crimson base.

Officers wore the same uniforms as the men, substituting silver in place of white on the uniform and czapska. The pouch belt was the same with the addition of the ecusson, chains and crown decoration. The pouch would probably have the flap edged with silver and a silver eagle at the centre. Around the waist a silver sash was worn, which tied at the left.

The men and trumpeters had a cloth shabraque in amarante, edged with a white stripe and white piping. A cylindrical valise was carried, in amarante with white lacing (Plate 6). The girth was white and the surcingle grey or brown. All other horse straps and reins were black with iron buckles. The stirrups were of iron with white leathers. Officers had an amarante saddle cloth but with the stripe of silver. Senior officers had an additional stripe inside, half the width of the outer. The reins, etc, were decorated with silver studs and chainwork, and the buckles were also silver. White gauntlets were worn by all ranks, the men's having buff glove parts. As always the trumpeters rode greys.

An interesting figure is that of the kettle-drummer. The two drums had amarante drum banners edged and fringed with silver, bearing a silver eagle. The usual cloth shabraque was carried with a wide silver stripe. The drummer himself wore Oriental style dress as was the fashion for mounted drummers at the time. The czapska, the same as the men's, was encircled around the base by a white turban which fastened with a silver clip at the front. No plate or peak appeared. The plume was white with a crimson base and no cords or flounders were worn. A collarless amarante jacket was worn with silver lace edging to the neck and the front. The sleeves were encircled with 10 silver lace bands. Over the jacket a white surcoat was worn. This garment was sleeveless and came to mid-thighs or even a little lower. The neck folded open in a 'V' and the turned back part of the surcoat had a silver lace edging. A silver sash was worn around the waist and tied on the left. The baggy trousers were coloured amarante. Horse straps, etc, were the same as the men's. The stirrups were of the open-box type, as shown above. A mameluke sword was slung on white cords around the shoulder (Plate 9), the sword and scabbard being of brass. Gauntlet gloves, as worn by the men, were also worn by the kettle-drummer. On campaign a medium grey single-breasted blouse was worn.

Chevaux Legers de Berg (Lancers de Berg)

LEFT TO RIGHT: Lancer of Elite Company in campaign dress. Note cords fastened round chest and plain-topped boots. Trumpeter in campaign dress wearing Imperial Livery, 1813. Lancer in campaign dress in Spain; shako was amarante with white lace top and bottom. Lancer in full dress; note braided cords hung across front of czapska and flounders hanging on right side.

This fastened with nine cloth buttons and had an amarante coloured collar. *Pantalon à cheval* were also grey with an amarante stripe, on which rode 18 white metal buttons. The czapska was covered with a black oilskin and a grey overcoat was usually slung over the right shoulder.

Lancers de Berg: After incorporation into the Guard the basic uniform colour became dark green with amarante facings.

In Spain this regiment wore a chasseur coatee with an amarante collar, cuffs, piping and turnbacks, and plain green pantalons with leather inserts. From the white Hungarian sword belt was carried a sabre, which appears to have been the three bar Guard style. The hilt was brass and the scabbard iron. An amarante shako with white lace top and bottom was worn. At the front a brass lozenge plate appeared below the red and white cockade. The plume was white, but no cords were worn.

The full dress uniform for this period was identical in style to that worn previously, except that now the basic colour of the kurtka and the trousers was green (Plate 3). The collar, lapels and cuffs (coloured amarante) were piped white. The horse furniture was the same as before.

For normal dress a white sheepskin saddle cloth was used with amarante vandyking around the edge. The kurtka was often worn with crossed-over lapels. Green pantalons with an amarante stripe and 18 white metal buttons were donned on the march, as was an oilskin cover to protect the czapska.

Plain green breeches and calf-length black leather boots were also worn.

zapskas

Lancer NCO

1

2

Officer Trumpeter

4

5

3

8

7

6

Plate 1: 1st Polish Lancers of the Guard

1. Kurtka, senior officer, full dress. 2. Trumpeter, 1807–10. 3. Trumpeter, 1810–15. 4. Brigadier, sleeve. 5 Fourrier, sleeve. 6. Kurtka, lancer. 7. Trumpet banner, both sides. 8. Kurtka, Marechal des Logis Chef.

Élite companies were now established and were distinguished by red epaulettes and a scarlet plume to the czapska. Centre companies wore green pointed shoulder straps piped amarante and white plumes. *Élite* companies are shown wearing a black busby with an amarante 'bag' and a scarlet plume (page 30). The carbine was issued and carried strapped to the left side of the saddle or hung from the carbine belt. The lance, issued in 1809, had a pennon with amarante over white.

Trumpeters from 1812 wore the Imperial livery. This appeared in the form of seven inverted chevrons on the arms and as edging to the collar, lapels, cuffs and turnbacks. The lapel buttonholes also had brandenbergs in Imperial lace. Epaulettes were white. Basic uniform colour for trumpeters were the same as 'the other ranks', green with amarante facings. The czapska had a green upper part, piped white, but was otherwise identical to that already described. Any of the leg wear described could be worn by the trumpeters. The trumpeter's sheepskin was black and he invariably rode a grey horse.

Tartares Lithuaniens

The *Tartares Lithuaniens* wore an Oriental style of uniform which varied greatly from man to man. We can, therefore, only give a broad outline of the general appearance. A black astrakhan-covered shako was worn with the bottom encircled by a yellow turban. A green 'bag' hung to the right and had a red tassel. The peak was edged with brass and in place of a shako plate, three stars appeared over a crescent, all in brass. A green long-sleeved jacket was worn over which was a red sleeveless, unbuttoned waistcoat (Plate 3). The waistcoat had no collar and was ornamented with yellow lace. The collar of the jacket was red with yellow lace. Trousers were baggy and these had a red stripe on the outer seams. The square saddle cloth was either red laced yellow, or green laced red. Single holster covers were carried on the saddle matching the saddle cloth colour. A crowned eagle of the stripe colour appeared in the rear corners and a crowned 'N' in the same colour on the holster covers (Plate 6). The saddle itself was of the high Eastern style shown in the drawings. The cylindrical valise was identical in colour to the saddle cloth, with lacing also as carried on the saddle cloth. The lance pennon was red over green or white. Officers had gold in place of yellow and wore a white plume in a gilt tulip holder. Also a gold tassel hung at the rear corners of the saddle cloth. Cloaks were white or pale grey. Further variations included yellow jacket, white plume on shako, red trousers with a yellow stripe, blue jacket with blue collar, blue trousers with yellow stripe, shako with a blue turban bearing narrow yellow bands, blue 'bag' with yellow tassel, and a white over red plume.

A second-style uniform was introduced in 1813 but, until the time the unit was absorbed by the *3eme Eclaireurs*, both types of uniform were worn. Basically the new uniforms consisted of a black fur colpack with a green 'bag', white cords and flounders and a red plume. The jacket was crimson with a yellow waistcoat which had black decorations. The baggy trousers were now blue without any stripe. The cylindrical valise was either crimson or grey, and a blue saddle cloth with pointed rear ends and devoid of ornamentation was used. The saddle itself was covered by a black sheepskin. The lance pennon now became crimson over white.

With all the styles described a white waist belt was worn with a brass plate, or, in place of this, a yellow sash tying to the left. A curved bladed dagger was

Tartares Lithuaniens

LEFT TO RIGHT: Later version of the uniform as worn by a lancer. Officer, showing extensive gold lacing. Lancer in first style of uniform.

carried in a black scabbard, which was thrust behind the belt or sash. The pouch belt was also white with a plain black pouch. Officers, however, had a black pouch belt, edged with gold as was the flap of the black pouch. In this case the flap also had a gilt eagle. There is some confusion as to the type of sword carried by this unit, but in keeping with its Oriental image one would presume that a mameluke style sword was favoured (Plate 9). Horse straps and reins were identical to those described for the Polish Lancers, with the exception that the open-box style stirrups were used and the officers had a large gold tassel hanging from the breast ornament, while the half-moon ornament strap around the neck was lined with red cloth that showed at the edges.

Records exist of the dress of two individual trumpeters and a trumpet-major of the *Tartares Lithuaniens*.

The first trumpeter wore a black astrakhan shako with a pale yellow turban encircling the lower half. At the front appeared a crescent surmounted by a star in gold. The flap or 'bag' on the top of the shako was dark green with yellow piping and a crimson tassel. The peak was of black leather, bound with brass. The chin scales were also brass. The under-jacket was sky blue with red lacing to the collar and pointed cuffs. The same lacing appeared on the front edge of the jacket and sky blue shoulder straps, piped red, passed over the

Czapskas

Lancer

Trumpeter

1

2

3

5

6

7

Plate 2: 2nd Dutch Lancers of the Guard
1. Kurtka, Marechal des Logis Chef. 2. Officer. 3. Trumpeter, full dress. 4. Trumpeter, service dress. 5. Lancer. 6. Fourrier. 7. Brigadier. 8. Trumpet Banner.

5

GARDE
IMPÉRIALE
L'EMPEREUR
DES FRANÇAIS
AU 2ᵐᵉ RÉGIMENT
DES CHEV. LÉGERS
LANCIERS

VALEUR
ET DISCIPLINE
1ᵉʳ ESCADRON

3

4

8

9

10

11

Plate 3
Key to numbers on page 65.

37

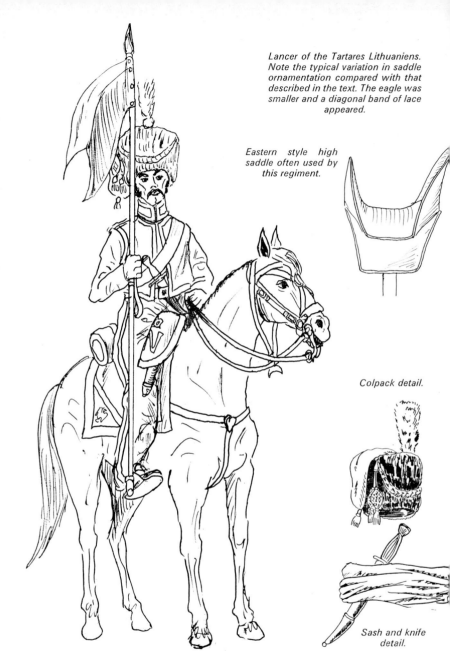

Lancer of the Tartares Lithuaniens. Note the typical variation in saddle ornamentation compared with that described in the text. The eagle was smaller and a diagonal band of lace appeared.

Eastern style high saddle often used by this regiment.

Colpack detail.

Sash and knife detail.

'bolero' waistcoat to fasten near the collar with a brass button. The waistcoat and baggy trousers 'a la mameluke' were dark red. The edges of the bolero waistcoat were laced yellow and on each side at the front were yellow lace Hungarian knots. The trousers had, on the outer seams, green lacing, piped with yellow. The waist belt and pouch belt were white, as already described. The trumpet was of brass with mixed green and red cords.

The second trumpeter wore the same style shako with the addition of a white plaited cord hanging across the front. Also at the top front was a white plume rising from a yellow pompom. No turban appears in this example and the tassel on the 'bag' was yellow in place of crimson. The under-jacket was yellow and the yellow collar was edged with two rows of crimson lace. The yellow pointed cuffs were edged with a single stripe of crimson lace, which formed a Hungarian knot at the point. The shoulder straps were yellow piped crimson. The 'bolero' was crimson with two yellow lace stripes at the edges. The remainder is the same as the first trumpeter, except that the first figure wore black boots and the second wore yellow leather boots.

The *Trompette-Major* wore a white astrakhan shako with a black peak, edged in brass, and brass chin scales. Around the lower portion a sky blue turban with narrow vertical gold stripes was worn and this fastened at the front by means of a gold band. The crescent and star appeared in gold at the front. The 'bag' was sky blue with yellow or gold piping and a crimson tassel. The jacket was sky blue with a gold lace stripe down the front and on the collar, which was piped on either side in crimson. The sky blue pointed cuffs were edged in a like manner. There also appeared above each cuff an inverted 'V' chevron of gold lace piped crimson. The bolero waistcoat was crimson with two gold lace stripes, separated by a crimson line, around the edges. The trousers were sky blue with gold Hungarian knots at the front and crimson stripes, edged gold, on the outer seams. The boots were of yellow leather and the belts were white. The trumpet, in this instance, was silver with crimson cords.

The last three regiments of Lancers of the Guard were the three regiments of *Eclaireurs* or Scout Lancers. Whilst forming one Corps, the regiments had different uniforms. Surviving records of these regiments are scanty and, therefore, certain gaps exist.

1st Regiment of Eclaireurs

The 1st Regiment had both Old and Young Guard sections. The Old Guard uniform was in hussar style with a dark green dolman and pelisse and white cords and braiding. The collar and cuffs of the dolman were scarlet with white lace edging. A crimson sash with white barrels was worn. For full dress wear scarlet hussar breeches were worn with white stripes and spearheads. This dress order was rare as the regiment was on active service for the major part of its existence. The more usual dress was either green pantalons with a single scarlet stripe and white metal buttons, or plain grey pantalons with cloth-covered buttons. Both had black leather inserts.

It is logical to assume that officers had the same uniform but with silver in place of white and grey, or white fur to the pelisse in place of black. NCOs usually had brown fur on the pelisse.

The Young Guard section, which was in the majority, wore a green Habit Kinski with scarlet piping to the collar, cuffs and the front edge of the coat. Turnbacks were scarlet, with or without green eagles. Pointed shoulder straps were worn, green and piped scarlet. Buttons were white metal for the men and silver for officers. Leg wear was the same as the Old Guard. Both sections wore a black shako with a scarlet lace band around the top. At the front a brass eagle plate was carried below the cockade. The chin scales were brass and the peak was plain. Usually a scarlet pompom was worn but, no doubt, for full dress wear a plume would be added. Though no cords are shown on the reference

Chasseur
coatee,
Officer,
3rd Regiment ▶

Habit veste, 1st Regiment

Habit veste, Marechal des
Logis Chef, 5th Regiment

**Plate 4:
Line Cavalry**

Helmet,
6th Regiment,
Elite Company

Habit veste, Trumpeter,
Elite Company, 2nd Regiment

Officer's
helmet

Trumpeter, 6th Regiment,
Imperial livery coatee

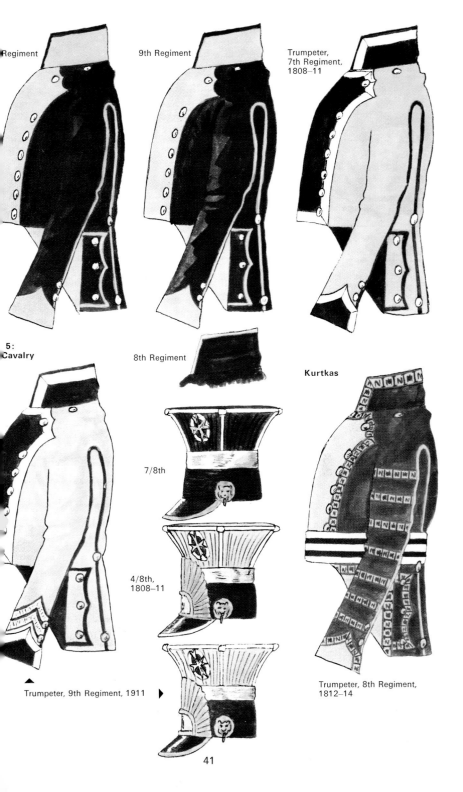

Regiment

9th Regiment

Trumpeter,
7th Regiment,
1808–11

5:
Cavalry

8th Regiment

Kurtkas

7/8th

4/8th,
1808–11

Trumpeter, 9th Regiment, 1911 ▶

Trumpeter, 8th Regiment,
1812–14

41

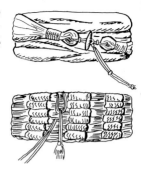

LEFT: Detail of eagle plate on shako of 1st Eclaireurs. RIGHT: Details of waist sash, Old Guard Section, 1st Eclaireurs.

material in the author's possession, one would assume that white cords would be used for full dress wear. It is presumed that officers wore the same headgear, possibly with the addition of silver cords.

A white pouch belt carried a black pouch with a brass eagle on the flap. Where the carbine was carried, a carbine belt was worn over the pouch belt. (The front rank was armed with the lance and the rear with the carbine.) A three-bar guard, light cavalry pattern sabre was carried in an iron scabbard. The hilt and carrying rings were brass and a white Hungarian sword belt was used. Officers possibly had red leather pouch belts and pouches, with the flap edges and belt edges in gold. The Hungarian sword belt would, in this case, also be red with gold edging. Sword knots for the men were white and probably silver lace for the officers.

The horse furniture consisted of a green cloth shabraque with scarlet piping at the extreme edge and a stripe of white inside it. In the pointed corner, a white crowned eagle was carried. Officers probably substituted silver for white. A cylindrical valise was carried, green with scarlet piping and white lace. Officers wore the same as the Old Guard section. Horse strappings and reins, etc, were of black leather. The girth was white and the surcingle was grey. Stirrups were of iron and the stirrup leathers appear to have been black (Plate 6).

2nd Regiment of Eclaireurs

The 2nd Regiment wore a chasseur coatee, Habit Kinski, in green cloth with crimson collar, cuffs and turnbacks (Plate 3). The collar was piped green and the front edge of the coat was piped crimson. Pointed shoulder straps were green with crimson piping. Buttons were of white metal. Leg gear was the same as described for the 1st Regiment, but with crimson in place of scarlet. It has been difficult to discover any positive record of officers' uniforms at the time of writing, however.

A crimson cylindrical shako was worn by the other ranks, with either brass chin scales or a black leather chinstrap. The cockade was carried at the front, slightly above the midway point and an aurore cord strap came from the top of the shako to a white metal button in the centre of the cockade. A half-round pompom in green appears at the front of the shako, the flattened part against the shako and half appearing above the shako top (Plate 3). A yellow cord fastened to a button at the top rear and passed in a loop over one shoulder and under the arm at the other side.

Again legwear consisted of crimson hussar breeches with yellow stripes for

Eclaireurs

LEFT TO RIGHT: Man of the Old Guard Section, 1st Regiment. Man of the Young Guard Section, 1st Regiment, campaign dress. Man of the 2nd Regiment, campaign dress. Rear view of officer of 1st Regiment in the full dress uniform of the Old Guard Section. See also drawings on page 46.

full dress wear, but this was probably never worn. The usual wear consisted of green overalls with two crimson stripes, no buttons or leather inserts, green pantalons with a single crimson stripe, 18 white metal buttons, black leather inserts and angled pockets, piped crimson with three white metal buttons or grey pantalons with a single crimson stripe and 18 white metal buttons.

Horse furniture followed the same pattern as the 1st Regiment, but with a yellow stripe and green piping to the edge of the shabraque and yellow eagles in the corners. The cylindrical valise was crimson with yellow lacing. Belts and equipment were the same as the 1st Regiment.

3rd Regiment of Eclaireurs

The 3rd Regiment wore an identical uniform to the 1st Polish Lancers, to whom they were attached, with the following differences.

In place of the plume a white pompom was carried on the czapska, and cords and flounders were not worn. Around the waist a white sash or girdle was worn which had two blue stripes. In place of the epaulettes they wore blue pointed shoulder straps, piped white. The shabraque was blue without stripes or piping, but with a white eagle in the rear corners. It would appear that plain grey overalls were the only legwear used. These probably had 18 cloth-covered buttons down the outside seams, but no leather inserts.

All the *Eclaireur* regiments had the lance pennon crimson above white.

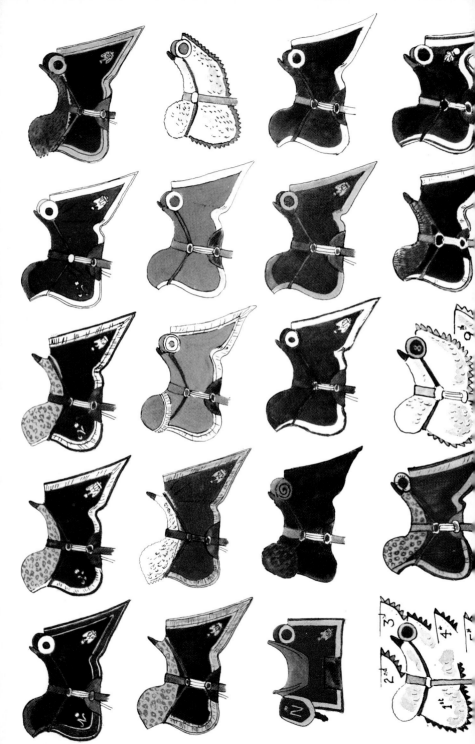

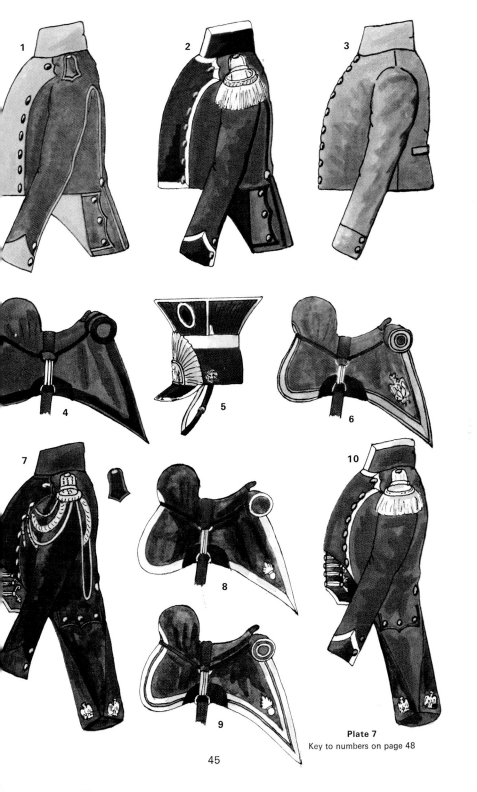

Plate 7
Key to numbers on page 48

45

Mounted lancer of the 2nd Regiment of Eclaireurs. Note the cord from the button at the top of the shako looped around the neck. For a front view of the cylindrical shako see page 9.

Inset views, above left, show details of pelisse and dolman lace and fastenings for 1st Eclaireurs Old Guard Section. See figure drawings on page 43.

4: Lancer Regiments of the Line

THERE were nine Lancer Regiments of the Line. We will look at the 1st to the 6th Regiments and the 7th to 9th Regiments separately.

Chevau-Legers Lanciers Francais Regiments. 1 to 6

HEADGEAR

A brass helmet identical in shape to the previous dragoon helmet but with the addition of a small rear peak was worn. The lower part was covered by a band of dark fawn fur with brass chin scales attached by circular rosaces, embossed with a five-pointed star. The front and the rear peaks were of black leather, the front one being bound with brass. In place of the horsehair hanging down at the back, a black horsehair crest was worn. A brass holder was attached just ahead of the left rosace and a scarlet plume worn in this on full dress occasions. For normal, or service wear, the helmet was without a plume but, in some instances, a lentile disc was worn in the squadron colour.*
(Plate 4).

The 6th Regiment *élite* company wore a crest of scarlet with a white plume.

Trumpeters would appear to have worn, at least at the onset, white crests with scarlet plumes, though at later dates they appear with black crests, except the 6th Regiment which had scarlet.

Officers wore a different shaped helmet, as shown in Plate 4, with the lower part and both peaks covered in panther skin. It would appear that officers hardly ever wore a plume and the crest was always black. Note that the lower edge of the officer's helmet was trimmed all around with brass.

COATS

The Habit Veste worn by the men was dark green with pointed cuffs. The collar, lapels, cuffs, turnbacks and piping to the shoulder straps and pockets were of the facing colour as shown below.

Regiment	Facing Colour
1st	Scarlet
2nd	Aurore
3rd	Rose
4th	Crimson
5th	Sky Blue
6th	Gorance Red

Two types of pocket were worn, the three-pointed vertical pocket and the

*1st Red, 2nd Sky blue, 3rd Aurore and 4th Violet

47

ABOVE: This diorama shows Marshal Prince Poniatowski, C-in-C of the Polish Armies (left), followed by a Polish Guard Lancer and a trumpeter of the same regiment (Historex models). BELOW, LEFT: An officer of the 7th or 8th Regiment of Polish Line Lancers (photos courtesy Lynn Sangster). BELOW, RIGHT: Detail of top of czapska and some details of the lettering and decoration of the standards.

Plate 8

Key to Plate 7, page 45

30th Chasseurs Lanciers (top two rows). 1. Kurtka. 2. Trumpeter's kurtka. 3. Stable dress. (All worn with red pantalons à cheval with black leather inserts.) 4. Shabraque, lancier and trumpeter. 5. Czapska. 6. Shabraque, officer. Lanciers Gendarmes (bottom two rows). 7. Habit coat, officer. 8. Shabraque, other ranks. 9. Shabraque, officers (silver lace). 10. Habit coat, trumpeter.

Chevau Legers Francais, Regiments 1-6

LEFT TO RIGHT: Carabinier in campaign dress. Marechal des Logis of Elite Company in full dress. Lancer of Centre Company in full dress. Officer in full dress.

Soubisse pocket (Plate 4).

On service the lapels were crossed over so that the facing colour only appeared as a narrow piping on the right-hand side. The collar was sometimes piped dark green. *Élite* companies wore full epaulettes of red and the turnbacks of all companies carried a dark green eagle. For details of rank distinctions see Appendix 4.

At first a dark green cloak was issued but this was replaced by a dark green overcoat with a cape on the shoulders. On campaign the coat was often carried rolled over the left shoulder, the ends fastened together at the right hip by a leather strap.

Trumpeters: There exists some confusion as to what uniforms were worn by the trumpeters. Under the 1811 regulations the Imperial livery would be worn, but it is possible that at first the system of wearing reversed colours applied. Documentary evidence suggests that the *élite* companies of the 1st and 2nd Regiments wore coats of dark blue with the normal facing colours. However, the collar, lapels and cuffs were edged with white lace, and white epaulettes were worn. A scarlet trumpet banner, fringed with gold and with a gold crowned eagle on both faces was carried. It is possible that yellow lace also adorned the collar, lapels and cuffs where reversed colours were worn. Shoulder straps would be of the facing colour, piped dark green, like the pockets (Plate 4).

After 1812 the Imperial livery was worn on the chasseur coat by all

49

Chevau Legers Francais, Regiments 1-6

LEFT TO RIGHT: Officer wearing trousers with a gold edged stripe as described in text. Officer in campaign dress; note that he is wearing enlisted men's breeches and helmet. Trumpeter of 5th Regiment in chasseur coatee with an unusual lace; this was mixed red and white. (The collar, cuffs, turnbacks, and piping were all sky blue. The coat and breeches were green. The breeches and boots had yellow lace and the helmet crest was white.) Lancer in stable dress.

regiments, with the collar, cuffs and turnback edged with the lace and with five horizontal double stripes across the chest. Seven inverted chevrons adorned the sleeves. The collar, cuffs and turnbacks were of the facing colour and either eagles or crowned 'N's appeared on the turnbacks.

It is difficult to say with any degree of certainty what form the shoulder straps took as contemporary prints show both three-pointed straps piped with facing colour, and white (red for *élite* companies) full epaulettes.

Officers: The officers wore the usual Habit Veste either with the lapels folded back or crossed over. When crossed over, buttoning on the left, the top button was left undone and folded back across the chest to form an ecusson of the facing colour. Epaulettes and contra epaulettes were worn, as Appendix 4. The collar was sometimes piped dark green. A chasseur coatee was also worn on service with collar, cuffs and the front edge piped in the facing colour.

TROUSERS AND BOOTS

Men: Full dress wear consisted of dark green hussar style breeches with a yellow stripe at the side seams, joining across the seat with a ring below.

At the front Regiments 1, 2 and 4 had yellow spearhead decorations, and Regiments 5 and 6 had Hungarian knots. It is uncertain as to the exact style worn by the 3rd Regiment.

Boots were of black leather, hussar style, with yellow trimming and tassels.

On service a variety of *pantalons à cheval* were worn. Some examples were

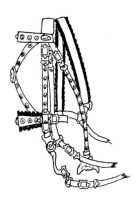

LEFT: Trumpeter of the Chevau Legers Francais wearing Imperial Livery on his coatee. The uniform shown was worn on campaign. In full dress hussar style breeches would be worn. ABOVE: Trumpet banner of Chevau Legers Francais. It had a scarlet ground and gold lace eagle and fringe. ABOVE, RIGHT: Halter and rein arrangement for officers. The cloth lining was not used by all regiments.

of grey cloth with the inside legs of black leather and the bottoms to the height of the hussar boots completely of leather. These fastened at the sides with 18 cloth-covered buttons (black leather buttons on the leather parts). A second style was dark green overalls with black leather inside legs and bottoms, and two stripes of the facing colour on the outside seams, separated by green piping. A variation of this featured a single line of piping of the facing colour down the outside seams.

Officers: Officers wore basically the same style of breeches as the men, but with stripes and decorations in gold braid. The boots were also trimmed with gold. The decoration at the front of the breeches was in the form of spearheads and the actual number of stripes varied according to rank (see Appendix 4).

When the chasseur coatee was worn in service, the officers sometimes wore the same decoration on the breeches front as the men (ie, either spearheads or Hungarian knots, depending on the regiment). Pantalons were similar to the men's but usually without the leather inserts, and they were sometimes in the facing colour with a thin gold stripe on either side of 18 gilt buttons down the outside seam.

STABLE DRESS

Stable dress for the men consisted of a plain dark green vest with long sleeves, fastened down the front with 10 brass buttons. The cuffs each fastened with two brass buttons and one appeared on each shoulder strap. Trousers were a creamy linen and the headgear consisted of a dark green forage cap with a yellow stripe piped at the edge with the facing colour. The pointed flap was also piped with the facing colour.

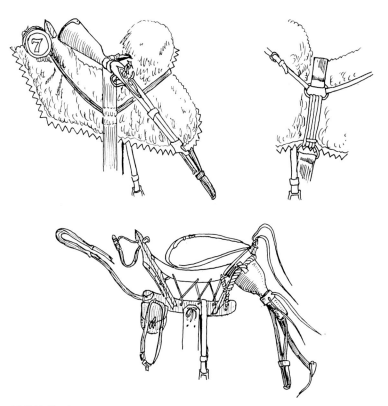

ABOVE: The frame of wood and leather which was used under the sheepskin saddle cloth. The strap which attached to the lower piece and passed under the horse was known as the girth strap. TOP LEFT: The sheepskin is shown in place and the method of attaching the carbine can be seen. Note the strap around the butt passing through a slit in the sheepskin. The strap passing over the sheepskin was called the surcingle. TOP RIGHT: Method of fastening the surcingle.

EQUIPMENT

Men: With the exception of the 6th Regiment all belts were of whitened leather with black leather pouches. *Élite* companies had a brass grenade on the flap while centre companies had the flaps plain. The waist belt had an oblong plate, either plain or bearing a grenade, with a crowned 'N' or an eagle. The shoulder belt and carbine belt had brass buckles and in the case of most *élite* companies a brass grenade appeared on the shoulder belt at the front. The 6th Regiment had ochre-coloured leather equipment. At first the sabre had a single bar guard but was quickly superseded by the three-bar version. In both cases the hilt was brass and the scabbard steel. A white sword knot was used by centre companies and *élite* companies had the fringes of the tassel in red. Where issued the carbine was either suspended on the carbine belt or carried on the right-hand side of the saddle. A white canvas cover was normally fitted over the firing mechanism when the weapon was strapped to the saddle. Where a carbine was issued a bayonet was carried on the waist belt in a brown leather scabbard.

Spurs were of blackened steel, except for officers who had silver. The officers' sabres were essentially the same as the men's, but with a gilt guard and gilt swivel rings on the steel scabbard. The sword knot was gold. Officers wore a red Moroccan leather pouch belt with five gold stripes. The pouch was gilded with a black leather flap, edged gold and carrying a gold eagle, a crowned 'N', or crossed lances. A variation on the above was a plain red belt, edged gold. On the chest a gold shield bearing an 'N' was connected by three gilt chains to a gold crown above. The waist belt was of red Moroccan leather with five gold stripes and fastened by an oblong plate of gold, usually carrying an embossed eagle. An alternative was a Hungarian waist belt of red leather, edged gold. In both cases the sword slings were red, edged gold (see Plate 10). On service a plain black Hungarian sword belt was sometimes worn.

Trumpets were of brass with white cords and tassels, except in the *élite* companies where they were red. The square trumpet banners were green, fringed gold and bearing a crowned eagle embroidered in gold in the centre. *Élite* companies had banners of scarlet.

Gauntlet gloves were buff with white gauntlets, except in the 6th where they were ochre. Officers are often shown wearing black gauntlet gloves.

The lance was of blackened wood with a scarlet over white pennon. For the 6th Regiment the strap was ochre, for all others white.

HORSE FURNITURE

Other ranks had a full sheepskin of white, edged with vandyking of the facing colour, but trumpeters had black sheepskins. A green cylindrical valise was carried with yellow lace at the ends. In some cases the regimental number appeared in yellow also. All straps were black with blackened steel buckles. The girth was a pale grey, but was almost obscured by the black surcingle. Blackened steel stirrups were hung on buff leather straps. The disc on the horse's forehead, the heart on its chest and the crescent hanging below the neck were of brass, the disc and heart bearing the regimental number.

Officers had a green cloth shabraque with pointed ends. The edge was laced gold and piped green. The seat was covered by panther skin and the valise had gold lace. The leading rein bridle was backed by red cloth, which showed at the edges. Buckles on the bridles were of brass and brass studs decorated the cross straps and harness. Stirrup leathers were white.

Regiments 7 to 9 and Vistula Legion

As detailed in Part 1, the *7eme* and *8eme Chevau Legers Lanciers Polonais de Ligne* were formed from the two regiments of the Vistula Legion, and the 9th from the *30eme Chasseurs*.

HEADGEAR

While serving a part of the Vistula Legion the czapska was primrose yellow (hereafter referred to as yellow) with a black turban and no centre lace. The yellow top was piped white. The French cockade was superimposed by a white metal Polish cross and in full dress a white plume was worn. The brass

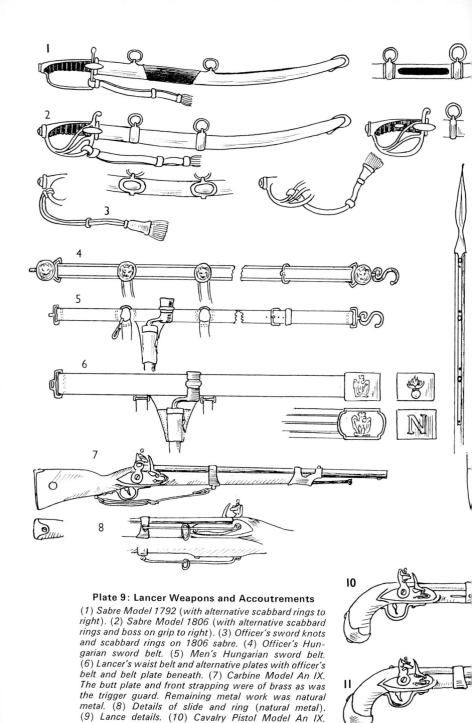

Plate 9: Lancer Weapons and Accoutrements

(1) Sabre Model 1792 (with alternative scabbard rings to right). (2) Sabre Model 1806 (with alternative scabbard rings and boss on grip to right). (3) Officer's sword knots and scabbard rings on 1806 sabre. (4) Officer's Hungarian sword belt. (5) Men's Hungarian sword belt. (6) Lancer's waist belt and alternative plates with officer's belt and belt plate beneath. (7) Carbine Model An IX. The butt plate and front strapping were of brass as was the trigger guard. Remaining metal work was natural metal. (8) Details of slide and ring (natural metal). (9) Lance details. (10) Cavalry Pistol Model An IX. (11) Cavalry Pistol Model An XIII.

A lancer of 7th, 8th, or 9th Regiments, Centre Company. Note the pantalons à cheval. Sheepskin on saddle, and the waist girdle, distinguished the line lancers from guard lancers (Historex model).

chin chain was hooked on to brass lions' heads on either side. The black leather peak was plain and no plate was carried. When formed into the 7th Regiment of the Line, the czapska was dark blue with a black turban and white braid in the middle (these details also apply to the 8th and 9th Regiments). The top was piped white and again had the white metal Polish cross on the cockade. The peak now appears to have been trimmed with white metal or brass. The chin chain remained unchanged.

From 1811 the usual lancer sunray plate in brass with the white metal centre appeared. Centre companies did not wear cords or flounders, and in place of the plume a carrot-shaped pompom was worn in the squadron colour: Red—1st, Sky blue—2nd, Aurore—3rd, Violet—4th. The élite companies wore a red plume and white cords and flounders (Plate 5).

Trumpeters: Trumpeters wore a yellow-topped czapska in the 7th and 8th Regiments, and a buff-topped czapska in the 9th. Both had white piping and details as for the other ranks. Plumes were white for centre companies and white over crimson for élite companies. In 1812 with the advent of the Imperial livery, the czapska were identical to the men's but the élite companies now wore red plumes.

Officers: The officer's czapska was identical to the other ranks, but in place of the white piping and white centre lace band, silver was worn. The cords and flounders were also silver.

Uniforms: The Vistula Legion Lancers wore a dark blue kurtka with facings and piping of yellow. Centre companies wore pointed shoulder straps of blue, piped yellow while the élite companies wore white epaulettes on the right shoulder and a white aiguillette on the left. A white girdle was worn

ABOVE, LEFT TO RIGHT: Lancer of the Vistula Legion, Centre Company, campaign dress, 1808-10. Lancer of 7th, 8th, or 9th Polish Lancer Regiment of the Line, Elite Company, full dress. Officer of Polish Line Lancers, full dress.

around the waist with two blue lines. For full dress wear blue trousers were worn with two stripes of yellow separated by blue piping. The *pantalons* à *cheval* were also blue with black leather inserts and a single stripe of yellow at the outside seam upon which rode 16 white metal buttons.

A grey cloak was worn and on campaign often rolled and slung over the right shoulder, the ends being strapped together at the left waist.

7th, 8th and 9th Regiments (after 1813)

The 7th and 8th Regiments wore an almost identical uniform to the Vistula Legions, except that in place of the plain yellow collar the 7th had yellow with blue piping and the 8th had blue with yellow piping. The 9th had a blue kurtka with facings of buff and the collar was buff piped blue. Centre companies had pointed shoulder straps piped with the facing colour and *élite* companies white (red for the 9th) epaulettes on the right and a white (or red) aiguillette on the left. Trousers and *pantalons* à *cheval* were as for the Vistula Legion but with buff in place of yellow for the 9th.

Trumpeters: Until 1812 the trumpeters wore kurtkas of reversed colours

Lancer in full dress, Centre Company, 8th Regiment of Polish Line Lancers (8eme Lanciers Polonnais de Ligne).

TOP LEFT: Lancer of Polish Line Lancers, Centre Company, campaign dress, 1811-14.
ABOVE LEFT: Trumpeter of Polish Line Lancers, Elite Company, in full dress with kurtka and lace of Imperial Livery.

Right side view of a lancer of the Centre Company of a Polish Line Lancer Regiment showing pointed epaulette, sheepskin on saddle, and absence of cap lines and flounders (Historex model).

(see Plate 5). In addition they wore white lace edging to the collar, lapels and cuffs. White epaulettes were worn by all companies, the *élite* companies being distinguished by a red half-moon on the epaulette. The trousers and overalls were the same as for the men. In 1812 the Imperial livery was introduced and the kurtka became dark green with facings and piping the same colour as the other ranks. The collar, cuffs, lapels, pockets and turnbacks were now edged with the Imperial lace and the sleeves had seven horizontal bars of lace (see Plate 5).

The girdle was still white with two blue bands. The trousers or overalls were now dark green with stripe(s) of the facing colour. Centre companies had pointed shoulder straps of green piped with the facing colour. *Élite* companies wore white epaulettes and aiguillettes. Buttons for men and trumpeters were of white metal.

Officers: Officers wore identical kurtkas and trousers to the men but upon their shoulders wore silver epaulettes of rank (see Appendix 4). The waist sash was of woven silver with two blue stripes. Senior officers (ie, Colonel or Major) had silver stripes on their trousers. Buttons were silver.

EQUIPMENT

The men wore a whitened leather shoulder belt with a plain black leather pouch (not worn by Vistula Legion as no musket was carried). The buckles were of brass. When the musket was carried a carbine belt of whitened leather was worn over the shoulder belt, and held to it by a small brass stud at the chest. The buckles and swivel hooks were brass. A white Hungarian sword belt was worn with a brass 'S' clasp. The sabre, with a brass three-piece guard

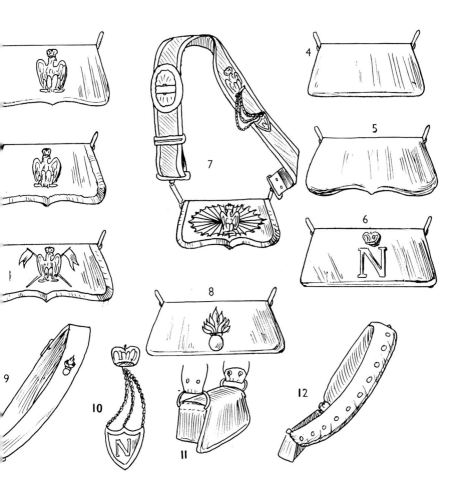

Plate 10: Pouch flaps and belts

(1) *1st Polish Lancers and 2nd Dutch Lancers.* (2) *Officer, 2nd Dutch Lancers.*
(3) *Officer, 7th-9th Lancers.* (4) *French Lancers of the Line, Young Guard, Dutch
Lancers, Tartares Lithuaniens, and Lancers de Berg.* (5) *Eclaireurs.* (6) *Alternative for
French Lancers of the Line.* (7) *Polish Lancers, officers.* (8) *French Lancers of the
Line, Elite Company.* (9) *Carbine belt of French Lancers of the Line, Elite Company.*
(10) *Alternative pouch belt decoration for officers.* (11) *View of pouch.* (12) *Officer's
pouch belt as worn in tenue de marche.*

on the hilt, was carried in an iron scabbard and the sword knot was white.
With the musket, of usual light cavalry pattern with brass metal work, a
bayonet was carried in a light brown scabbard suspended between the sword
slings. Pistols were carried under the sheepskin but in some cases, where no
musket was issued or carried, the pistol was suspended from the swivel hook
of the carbine belt (page 60). The lance had a black shaft with an iron point and
butt. The grip and loop were white and the pennon was white above crimson.
All centre companies wore white wrist gloves, while *élite* companies had

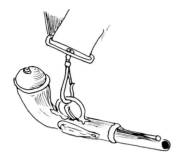

Method of carrying pistol from swivel clip-hook on carbine belt, as described in text.

white gauntlets. The trumpet was brass and had white cords and tassels for centre companies and red cords and tassels for *élite* companies. In 1812 all trumpet cords were mixed yellow and green. Trumpeters also wore white gloves (gauntlets for *élite* companies). Officers wore a black leather shoulder belt, ornamented with silver stripes or edges. On the chest a gold crown was worn above an ecusson (shield) below connected by three gold chains. The pouch itself was black with the flap edged silver and bearing a silver eagle superimposed over crossed lances (Plate 10).

A black Hungarian sword belt was worn with silver edging. The sabre had a gilt hilt and was carried in an iron scabbard with gilt fittings. The sword knot was silver. Gauntlet gloves were worn and were usually black, although white were used.

HORSE FURNITURE

Both the Vistula Legion and the 7th, 8th and 9th Regiments wore a white sheepskin saddle cover edged with vandyking of the facing colour. The cylindrical valise was dark blue with lace at the ends of the facing colour and from 1812 the regimental number, also in the facing colour, was carried at the ends. The bridles, and horse strappings, were of black leather with brass metal work. The girth was grey and the surcingle (which passed completely around the horse) was black. Stirrups were of blackened iron with black lance butts, and the stirrup leather white. The musket was carried on the right side of the saddle with the muzzle in a black leather boot and a brown leather strap passed around the small of the butt, then passed through the sheepskin to the pommel. A lock cover was usually fitted over the musket firing mechanism.

Trumpeters had the same horse furniture as the other ranks, but without the musket boot and lance butts. They rode grey horses, while the remainder rode horses of various colours.

Officers had a blue saddle cloth with pointed rear ends, piped with the facing colour and with a silver lace stripe inside the piping. The seat of the saddle was covered by black bearskin. The rubbing plate and surcingle were black and the girth white. Silver stirrups were hung on light brown leather straps. The bridles and reins (except the snaffle bridle) were of black leather with silver studs and buckles. The snaffle bridle and snaffle reins were covered with silver lace and the halter was lined with a vandyked cloth of the facing colour. Senior officers had a panther skin seat and an additional silver stripe on the saddle cloth, inside the usual stripe and half its width. No valise was carried by officers.

No standards appear to have been issued to the 7th, 8th and 9th Regiments, but the Vistula Legion standard is shown in Appendix 1.

30th Chasseurs à Cheval and the 9th Regt. (until 1813)

At the time of this regiment's formation as chasseurs in Hamburg there was a shortage in the stores at Hamburg of green cloth, the traditional material for chasseurs' uniforms. There was, however, an abundance of red cloth, a distinction that earned the regiment the name of the 'Red Lancers' (*Lanciers Rouges*) of Hamburg during the Russian campaign of 1812. The decision to arm the regiment with the lance probably accounted for the Polish style of dress.

Their headgear was the czapska with a red top, white band and black turban (see Plate 2). The top was piped white in the usual style. Contemporary prints show this regiment both with and without the 'sunray' plate. The black leather peak was bound with white metal and a black leather chin strap was worn. For full dress a black plume with a green top was worn, together with a white cord, plaited and attached to the top corners at each side of the czapska so that the cord hung across the 'sunray' plate. Officers had silver chin scales. The bicorne was worn quite extensively by officers, being plain black with a silver lace cockade strap and a white plume.

The kurtka was dark green with the collar, lapels, cuffs, turnbacks and piping in 'chamois' (a light yellow with a fawn tint). All the buttons were of white metal. The men wore pointed shoulder straps of dark green, piped chamois. Officers wore an identical kurtka but with silver buttons and silver epaulettes and contra epaulettes.

Trumpeters wore the same czapska as the men but their kurtka was red with

30eme Chasseurs Lanciers à Cheval

LEFT TO RIGHT: Lancer in campaign dress displaying lance and pennon, which was completely chamois in colour. Lancer wearing stable dress coat. Officer wearing pantalons à la Mameluke.

black facings. The black collar, lapels and cuffs carried a white lace edging. On the shoulders, white epaulettes were worn. Also worn was a stable vest which was buttoned down the front by nine white metal buttons and was a medium grey colour. The collar was chamois.

Both men and trumpeters wore red *pantalons à cheval* with a black stripe down the outside seams. The insides of the legs were reinforced by black leather inserts.

Officers favoured green baggy trousers, 'a la mameluke', either plain or with a chamois stripe, piped silver at the edges. Equipment was as already described for the 9th Regiment. The trumpet was brass with white cords.

The horse furniture for the men and trumpeters consisted of a red cloth shabraque with a black lace stripe around the edge. The extreme edge was piped red. The cylindrical valise was also red with black lace around the ends. Officers had a green shabraque with a chamois stripe edged both sides with silver piping. The outer piping being on the extreme edge of the shabraque. In the rear corners appeared a silver lace eagle. The valise was green with the same stripe as the shabraque. The pennon on the lance was coloured chamois.

By 1812 certain items began to appear in the regulation colours of the 9th Regiment, and it is possible that in this year the czapska, and later the kurtka, were blue. The red trousers were, however, in use until 1813 when the regiment was reformed and clothed in regulation style.

Lanciers Gendarmes

The *lanciers gendarmes* wore a black shako with a white metal eagle plate at the front. The black peak was edged with white metal and the chin scales were also of white metal. The shako of the trumpeters had the top encircled by a white lace band. Both officers and men wore a red plume, without a pompom, while the trumpeters had a white plume with a red pompom. Both officers and men wore a dark blue Habit Coat with long tails and pointed lapels and cuffs. The collar, cuffs and turnbacks were red and the lapels and horizontal pockets were piped red. Eagle motives appeared on the turnbacks, white for the men and silver for officers. The men had blue pointed shoulder straps, piped in red. Brigadiers were distinguished by two white inverted chevrons above each cuff, and *Marechal des Logis* and *Marechal des Logis Chefs* by one and two silver lace inverted chevrons respectively. The trumpeters, in contrast, wore a red Habit Coat with blue cuffs and turnbacks. The collar, lapels and cuffs were edged white with lace and the pockets piped blue. White full epaulettes were worn and white eagle motives on the turnbacks. The waistcoat was blue, laced white. Officers wore a silver contra epaulette on the left shoulder with silver aiguillettes and a silver-fringed epaulette on the right. Both officers and men wore a red waistcoat with three vertical rows of buttons, braided in white for the men and silver for the officer.

Men, trumpeters and officers wore blue breeches. The men and trumpeters had white Hungarian knot decorations at the front and white lace stripes on the outside seams. The officers had silver lace spearhead decorations indicative of rank and silver lace stripes. The men and trumpeters wore plain black hussar boots, while those of the officers were edged with silver.

All ranks wore whitened leather equipment, consisting of a pouch belt with a black pouch bearing a brass grenade on the flap and a white Hungarian sword belt. The sabre, light cavalry pattern with a single bar guard, had a brass hilt and was carried in a steel scabbard. Sword knot was white for the men and trumpeters and gold for officers. The men additionally wore a whitened leather carbine belt to which the carbine was usually attached. When not in this position the carbine was strapped at the left front of the saddle. The lance pennon was red over white. The trumpet was brass with red cords.

All ranks had a blue shabraque, the men having a single white stripe at the edges, the officers a silver stripe. Trumpeters had two slightly narrower white stripes. Men and trumpeters had a blue cylindrical valise, edged with lacing as worn on the shabraque. All ranks had a grenade in the rear corners of the shabraque, white for the men and trumpeters and silver for officers. The horse harness was the normal light cavalry style.

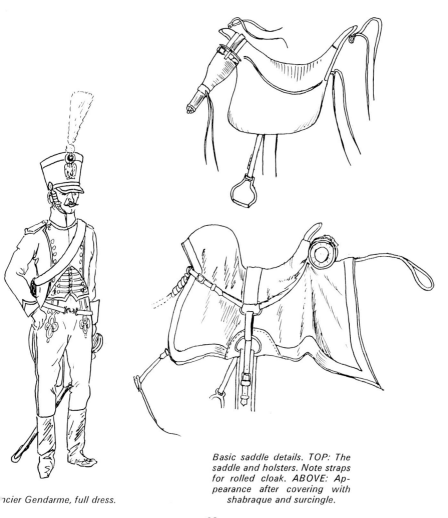

Basic saddle details. TOP: The saddle and holsters. Note straps for rolled cloak. ABOVE: Appearance after covering with shabraque and surcingle.

...icier Gendarme, full dress.

Appendix 1: Standards

OF the regiments covered in this volume, only the *1er Chevau Leger Lanciers Polonais de la Garde, 2eme Chevau Legers Lanciers de la Garde, 1er* to *6eme Regiments Chevau Legers Francais,* and the *Vistula Legion* appear to have been issued with standards.

The first type of standard used up to 1812 measured 60cm × 60cm and was carried on a blue staff 2m 10cm long and 3cm in diameter. On the top appeared a bronze eagle, as shown in Plate 3. The eagle, in fact, was the main feature and the standard itself of lesser impor. At first a standard was issued to each squadron, but eventually (1812?) only one standard was issued to the regiment as a whole. This standard had a white lozenge (Plate 3) with blue and red alternate corners. It was affixed to the staff by nine studs.

The 1st Polish Lancers were issued with this standard until 1812–13. On the face appeared, within the white lozenge, the following:

GARDE
IMPERIALE
L'EMPEREUR
DES FRANCAIS
AU 1er REGIMENT
DE CHEVAU LEGERS
LANCIERS

On the reverse:

VALER
ET DISCIPLINE
*ESCADRON

In each circlet appeared the figure 1 (one), the regimental number.

From 1813 a tricolour standard was carried. This measured 55cm × 55cm with a gold fringe 2,5cm wide. A tricolour cravat with gold fringes and embroidery was attached below the eagle by a gold cord. The total length of this cravat was 1m 20cm.

The details of the embroideries are shown in the drawing. The small decora-

* Number of squadron.

Tricolour standard of the 3rd Lancer Regiment.

Detail of Imperial Bee decoration.

tions are the Imperial bees and are shown in detail in the same drawing.
On the face appeared:

GARDE
IMPERIALE
L'EMPEREUR
NAPOLEON
AU 1er REGT
DE CHEVAU LEGERS
LANCIERS

On the reverse appeared the regiment's battle honours. The standard of the 2nd Regiment is shown on Plate 3. Details of the embroidery are shown in Plate 8.

The lettering on the standard used from 1813 was identical to the first with 2 substituted for 1.

The 1st to 6th Regiments of *Chevau Legers Francais* were issued with the tricolour standard, carried by the *élite* company of each regiment.

On the face appeared (in the case for the 3rd Regiment) the following:

L'EMPEREUR
NAPOLEON
AU 3me REGIMENT
DE CHEVAU LEGER
LANCIERS

On the reverse was:

ULM–AUSTERLITZ
JENA–EYLAU

The *Vistula Legion* standard was a beautiful sight. The coloured motifs were hand embroidered and the flag was of double thickness.

On the face the wording was in French. The top scroll read 'Republique Francais' and the lower 'Legion-Polonais'. At each corner the squadron number and the word 'Escadron' appeared. On the reverse the upper scroll read 'Rjeezypospolity Franconzkoy', the lower 'Legio Polskiey'. In the corners the wording was 'Swadron'. A spearhead, not an eagle, was fitted at the staff top.

In many cases with mounted units, the butt of the staff was carried in a boot attached to the stirrup, like the lance boots, and a belt, similar to a carbine belt with a swivel hook, was attached to a ring mounted on the staff to help support the standard.

In the case of the 1st and 2nd Lancers the standard was carried by a sous-lieutenant, and in the *Chevau Legers Francais* and the *Vistula Legion* by a senior Marechal des Logis Chef.

Key to Colour Plate 3, page 37
1. Czapska, Lancers de Berg. 2. Coatee, Lancers de Berg. 3. Shako, Tartares Lithuaniens. 4. Tartares Lithuaniens. 5. Standard of 2nd Dutch Lancers, face (top) and reverse. 6. Shako, 2nd Eclaireurs. 7. Coatee, 2nd Eclaireurs. 8. Shako, 1st Eclaireurs. 9. Dolman and pelisse of 1st Eclaireurs, Old Guard. 10. Detail of 2nd Dutch Lancers' standard. 11. Detail of standard decoration, 2nd Dutch Lancers.

Key to Colour Plate 6, page 44
Top row, left to right: (1st Polish Lancers) Lancer, Officer, Senior Officer, Trumpeter. (2nd Dutch Lancers) Lancer. **Second row, left to right:** (2nd Dutch Lancers) Officer, Trumpeter. (Lancers de Berg) Officer, Lancer, Lancer 1809–14, campaign dress. **Third row, left to right:** (Tartares Lithuaniens) Full dress, campaign dress—1st Eclaireurs, 2nd Eclaireurs, 3rd Eclaireurs. **Bottom row, left to right:** Chevau Leger Francais (1st to 5th Regiments), Polish Line Regiments (1st to 6th), Vistula Legion (7th, 8th, 9th), Officer, Polish Line Lancers, Gendarmier Lancer.

Appendix 2: Rank Equivalents

French		English
Colonel ⎱ Major ⎰ .. .. Senior Officers		⎰ Colonel ⎱ Lieutenant-Colonel
Chef d'Escadron		Major
Capitaine		Captain
Lieutenant		Lieutenant
Sous-Lieutenant		2nd Lieutenant
Marechal des Logis Chef ⎱ Marechal des Logis ⎰ Sous Officiers ..		⎰ Sergeant-Major ⎱ Sergeant
Fourrier		Quartermaster
Brigadier		Corporal
Soldat-Lancier		Private/Trooper
Trompette-Major		Trumpet-Major
Brigadier Trompette		Corporal Trumpeter
Trompette		Trumpeter

Appendix 3: Glossary

Aiguillettes	A cord shoulder strap with an ornamental knot from which loops of cord hung, fastening to the lapel buttonholes or to the chest.
Austrian knots	Decorative braids of interlacing circles appearing on cuffs. Sometimes used to refer to the ornamental loops on the front of hussar breeches (usually called Hungarian knots).
Barrel sash	A waist sash of cloth with three vertical rows of barrels of a contrasting colour.
Bicorne	A broad brimmed hat with the edges pinned up.
Bonnet de Police	Cloth service or fatigue cap usually with a pointed top which hung down or was tucked into the lower part.
Brass	Napoleonic brass was made with a high copper content resulting in a reddish appearance. Yellow brass was used in some instances.
Brandenburg	Lace edging to buttonholes usually with a fringe.
Carbine belt	(Or musket belt.) A leather shoulder belt with a swivel clip to which the carbine could be attached by a slide on the left side of the carbine.
Chevau Legers (Lanciers)	Light Horse (Lancers).
Chevrons	'V' shaped laces indicative of rank or service.
Colpak	A round fur hat usually with a cloth 'bag' hanging from the top.
Contra epaulette	Shoulder strap with the end wider than the other.
Cuff slash	Oblong patch on round cuffs which joined the cuff opening together with three or four buttons. Either plain or three pointed.
Czapska	Lancer cap of Polish origin, with square top.
Dolman	Tight fitting jacket of hussar pattern with varying numbers of braids across the chest.
Ecru	A creamy fawn shade of cotton.
Epaulette	As Contra epaulette but with fringes hanging from the rounded end.
Flounders	Flat woven oval shaped decorations with tassels at the bottom. Suspended by cords.
Girth	Wide band which held the saddle in place.
Grand tenue	Full dress.
Habit coat	Long or short tailed coat with a cutaway front.
Habit veste	Short tailed coat with a straight cut waist at the front.
Hungarian knots	Elaborate braiding of interwoven circles on the front of hussar breeches
Hussar boots	Soft leather boots curving up at the front and rear with a 'V' notch cut out at the front and a tassel hanging down from the 'V'.
Kurtka	A short jacket with only the front edges of the short tails turned back. Of Polish origin.

Lentile disc	A flattened disc of wool worn in place of the plume in later years of the Empire.
Pantalons à cheval	Trousers or leggings, usually with leather insides to the legs, worn over the breeches to protect them.
Pelisse	A fur trimmed jacket of hussar pattern slung over the left shoulder in summer and worn in place of the dolman in winter. Similar braids on the chest as those on the dolman.
Piping	A raised tubular length of material decorating the edges of pockets, cuffs, etc.
Pockets	Various style pockets were used, the main being three pointed and either vertical or horizontal.
Pointed lapels	Lapels which at the bottom followed the cutaway of the coat merging into the edge.
Pointed cuffs	Cuffs which rose to a point and buttoned at the rear, usually with one button on the cuff and one above.
Pompom	A spherical ball of wool worn in place of a plume.
Saddlecloth	Usually a square cut cloth worn under the saddle.
Sabretache	A leather case, usually with a coloured cloth face, suspended on three straps from the sword belt. Worn with hussar style uniform as the tightly fitted uniform did not include pockets.
Shabraque	A horse cloth which covered the saddle and usually had pointed rear ends hanging down.
Shako	A form of headgear made of leather and felt.
Shoulder strap	Self explanatory. Usually with a pointed (spear shaped) end but also plain.
Square cuffs	Cuffs which went horizontally around the sleeve. Normally worn with a cuff slash fastening.
Square lapels	Cutaway lapels which ended at an angle of 90° to the cutaway.
Surtout	A single breasted garment fastening with nine buttons. Usually worn as service dress.
Sword knot	Strap on the hilt of a sword which encircled the wrist to prevent loss in action. The end consisted of a knot and tassel.
Tenue de campaign	Dress worn when on active service in the field.
Tenue de marche	Dress worn when on the march. Sometimes identical to tenue de campaign.
Tenue de ville	Walking out dress.
Vandyking	Triangular edging usually to a sheepskin. Also called 'dogstooth'.
Velites	Recruits or trainees.
Waistcoat	Sleeveless garment worn under cutaway coat. Also with sleeves for fatigue duties in place of coat.
White metal	Natural metal colour.

Plate 11: Timbalier of the 1st Polish Lancers of the Guard

(illustration on next page)

This splendidly dressed mounted kettle-drummer wore a czapska with a crimson top with gold lines and piping. The centre band was gold with sky blue discs set around it. The bottom was of black fur. The flounders were gold. The plumes were two white and two crimson with the centre display white.

The under-jacket was crimson, buttoned down the front with gold buttons. The edges of the collar and front were laced gold as were the cuffs and the rear seams of the sleeves. Over this jacket, a white sleeveless smock was worn. The edge of the smock, down the front, around the collarless neck and at the shoulders was laced gold. At the bottom, two gold lace bands appeared separated by crimson. The back was split to the waist, so that the garment hung each side of the rider when mounted. From the rear shoulders false sleeves hung with gold lace at the sleeve ends. Around the waist a crimson sash with gold lines and fringes was knotted at the front.

The baggy trousers, tucked into short brown leather boots, were sky blue with a gold lace stripe. The mameluke sword in a black leather scabbard with gold hilt, sword knot and scabbard ornaments was slung over the right shoulder on crimson cords. The large horse cloth was crimson with ornate gold embroidery. The high-peaked saddle was of crimson leather with silver decoration. The brass drums had crimson drum banners with gold embroidery and fringes. The scroll, however, was silver as were the stars on the banner.

The horse straps were covered with gold scales, each with sky blue centres. The large discs had crimson centres and crimson tassels hung from them.

The horse plumes were identical to the czapska with two white and two crimson feathers and a white centre plume. The horse's mane was braided with crimson ribbons and a crimson rosette with gold fringes was worn over the tail. Reins were gold. The stirrups were the bucket type shown on page 31 and were gold.

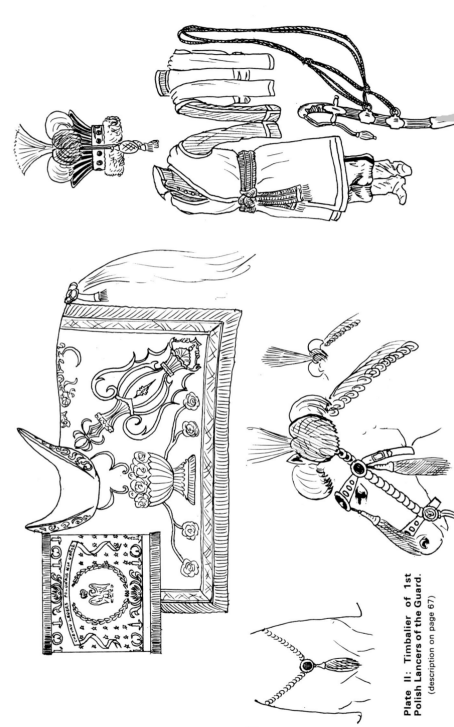

Plate II: Timbalier of 1st Polish Lancers of the Guard.

(description on page 67)

Appendix 4:
Ranks and Distinctions

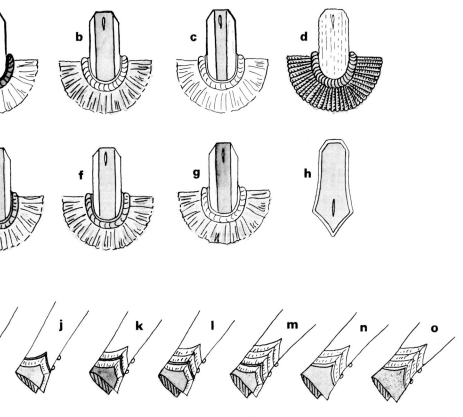

Plate 12: Rank distinctions

(a) 2nd Regiment, lancer. (b) 2nd Regiment, sous officier. (c) 2nd Regiment, officer. (d) 1st and 2nd Regiment, senior officer. (e) 2nd Regiment, velite. (f) 1st Regiment, Marechal des Logis. (g) 1st Regiment, Marechal des Logis Chef. (h) 2nd Regiment, Young Guard. (i) 1st and 2nd Regiment, trooper. (j) 1st Regiment, Brigadier. (k) 1st Regiment, Marechal des Logis and Trompette Brigadier. (l) 1st Regiment, Marechal des Logis Chef. (m) 1st Regiment, Trompette Major. (n) 2nd Regiment, Brigadier (yellow wool)and Marechal des Logis (gold lace). (o) 2nd Regiment, Marechal des Logis Chef.

(More rank distinctions on next page)

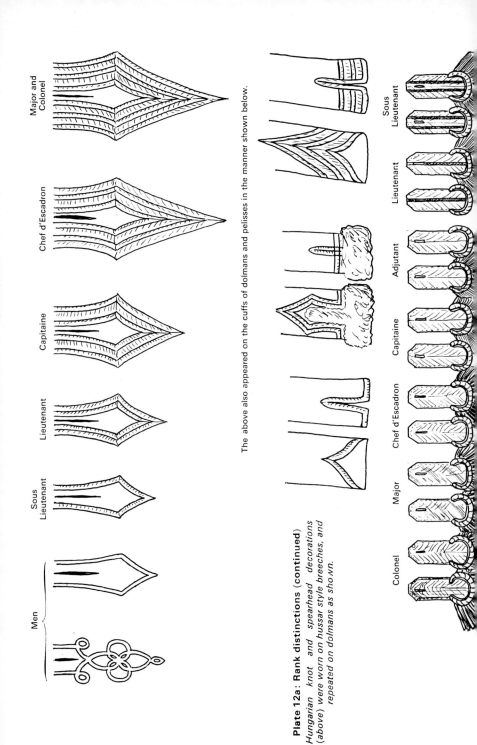

Major and Colonel

Chef d'Escadron

Capitaine

Lieutenant

Sous Lieutenant

Men

The above also appeared on the cuffs of dolmans and pelisses in the manner shown below.

Sous Lieutenant

Lieutenant

Adjutant

Capitaine

Chef d'Escadron

Major

Colonel

Plate 12a: Rank distinctions (continued)

Hungarian knot and spearhead decorations (above) were worn on hussar style breeches, and repeated on dolmans as shown.

Rank Distinctions: Officers

Rank	1st Polish Guard 1	2nd Dutch Guard 1	Lanciers de Berg 1	1st Eclaireurs Old Guard 3	1st Eclaireurs Young Guard	2nd Eclaireurs	French Line Regiments 4	Polish Line Regiments 1	Vistula Legion 1
Colonel	Silver epaulettes on both shoulders. Heavy bullion	As Polish Guard but gold	As Polish Guard	Five silver stripes on sleeves and breeches. 3 × 14mm, 2 × 23mm	As Polish Guard	As Dutch Guard	As Polish Guard	As Polish Guard	As Polish Guard
Major	As Colonel but shoulder straps gold. Heavy bullion	As Polish Guard but gold with silver shoulder straps	As Polish Guard	As Colonel but centre 14mm stripe in gold	As Polish Guard	As Dutch Guard	As Polish Guard	As Polish Guard	As Polish Guard
Chef d'Escadron	Silver epaulette on left shoulder. Contra epaulette on right. Heavy bullion	As Polish Guard but gold	As Polish Guard	Four silver stripes on sleeves and breeches. Alternate 14mm and 23mm	As Polish Guard	As Dutch Guard	As Polish Guard	As Polish Guard	As Polish Guard
Adjutant 2	As Chef d'Escadron but epaulette on right. Contra epaulette on left. Fine bullion	As Polish Guard but gold	As Polish Guard	—	As Polish Guard	As Dutch Guard	As Polish Guard	As Polish Guard	As Polish Guard
Capitaine	As Chef d'Escadron but fine bullion	As Polish Guard but gold	As Polish Guard	Two silver stripes of 14mm and a centre stripe of 23mm	As Polish Guard	As Dutch Guard	As Polish Guard	As Polish Guard	As Polish Guard
Lieutenant	As Capitaine but with a narrow red stripe on strap	As Polish Guard but gold	As Polish Guard	Two 14mm silver stripes	As Polish Guard	As Dutch Guard	As Polish Guard	As Polish Guard	As Polish Guard
Sous Lieutenant	As Capitaine but with two narrow red stripes	As Polish Guard but gold	As Polish Guard	One 14mm silver stripe on cuff	As Polish Guard	As Dutch Guard	As Polish Guard	As Polish Guard	As Polish Guard

NOTES:
1. Aiguilette, colour of epaulettes worn on right shoulder.
2. Aiguilette, colour of epaulettes worn on left shoulder
3. See Plate 12. For sleeve markings, the first 14mm stripe was on the cuff itself.
4. In addition, spearhead breeches stripes appeared as shown in Plate 12.

Rank Distinctions : NCOs and Trumpeters

Rank	1st Polish Guard	2nd Dutch Guard	Lanciers de Berg	1st Eclaireurs	2nd Eclaireurs	French Line Regiments	Polish Line Regiments	Vistula Legion
Marechal des Logis Chef	Silver lace edging to cuffs and two silver inverted chevrons above cuff 1	Two gold inverted chevrons above cuff 4	Two silver inverted chevrons above cuff 5	As Lanciers de Berg	As Dutch Lancers	As Dutch Lancers 6	As Dutch Lancers	Three inverted white chevrons above the cuffs
Marechal des Logis	As above but only one silver inverted chevron above cuff 2	One gold inverted chevron above cuff 4	One silver inverted chevron above cuff 5	As Lanciers de Berg	As Dutch Lancers	As Dutch Lancers 6	As Dutch Lancers	Two inverted white chevrons above the cuff
Farrier	As Brigadier plus inverted silver chevron on right upper arm 2	As Brigadier with one gold inverted chevron on right upper arm 4	As Dutch Guard but in silver	As Lanciers de Berg	As Dutch Lancers	As Dutch Lancers 6	As Dutch Lancers	—
Brigadier	Silver lace edging to collar, cuffs and lapels. As for Marechal des Logis Chef but three silver chevrons above cuff lace 1, 3	Two yellow inverted chevrons above the cuff 5	Two scarlet inverted chevrons above the cuff 5	As Lanciers de Berg	As Dutch Lancers	As Dutch Lancers 6	As Dutch Lancers	One inverted white chevron above the cuff
Trompette Major		Two gold inverted chevrons in addition to cuff lace. As 2 but in gold 5	As Dutch Guard but in silver 5					—
Brigadier Trompette	One silver inverted chevron in addition to cuff lace	One gold inverted chevron above cuff lace	As Dutch Guard but in silver					—
Service* Stripes	Silver for Marechals and Trumpeters, white for Brigadiers and men	Gold for Marechals and Trumpeters, yellow for Brigadiers and men	Silver Marechals and Trumpeters, scarlet for Brigadiers and men	As Lanciers de Berg	Gold for Marechals Scarlet for Brigadiers and men	Scarlet for all 7	Scarlet for all	

NOTES:

1. Aiguillettes were mixed silver and crimson. Ratio two silver to one crimson for Marechal des Logis Chef. Epaulettes had crimson straps, edged silver, silver half moons, mixed silver and crimson fringes. Silver lace edging to collar and lapels.
2. As Note 1 but crimson half moons. Aiguillettes ratio two crimson to one silver.
3. Two rows of silver lace to collar. Piping, cords and flounders on czapska in silver.
4. Aiguillettes were mixed gold and scarlet. Ratio two scarlet to one gold. Epaulettes had scarlet strap edged gold, gold half moons and mixed gold and scarlet fringes.
5. Cords on czapska and aiguillettes were mixed white and silver. Epaulettes had silver straps and half moons. Mixed white and silver fringes. Garde du Corp had silver in place of white edging for men to lapels, collar and cuffs. Trumpets as Garde du Corps.
6. In élite companies where epaulettes were worn, the half moon was gold. Shoulder strap was scarlet. In some cases fringes were mixed gold and scarlet. In others plain scarlet.
7. In certain cases N.C.O.s had gold stripes.

*One for 10-15 years' service, two for 20 years' service, three for 25 years' service.